John Fifteen Thirteen

John Nicholas Cassel

ISBN 978-1-64569-082-5 (paperback)
ISBN 978-1-64569-083-2 (digital)

Christian Faith Publishing, Inc.
832 Park Avenue
Meadville, PA 16335
www.christianfaithpublishing.com

Printed in the United States of America

For my beautiful wife, Kim. I couldn't have picked a stronger, more independent woman with whom to spend my life. She's exactly who I needed. Anyone else would have given up and walked out a long time ago. It's also for our son and daughter, Nick and Alex, the lives Kim and I created together. The three of them have supported me through many struggles, and I'm so blessed to have them.

I would like to thank my parents. I could not have done any of this without the values they instilled in me. I also wish to thank the rest of my family and close friends who worried and prayed for me every day I was deployed. Those thoughts and prayers brought me home at the end of every trip. Thank you all for the love and support.

Most of all, this book is for the family members and friends I've lost throughout the years.

He will wipe away every tear from their eyes, and death shall be no more.

Greater love has no one than this: to lay down one's life for one's friends.

—John 15:13 (NIV)

Foreword

This collection of stories is about overcoming life's challenges through faith. Not just faith in God but also faith in country, family, and friends. It's about facing adverse circumstances and not backing down, however bleak things may seem.

It's not about avoiding failures; those are inevitable. We all fall short of our own expectations sometimes. When life knocks you down, don't let it knock you out. Get back up, and keep fighting. It's about learning from your mistakes and using the lessons learned to do better next time.

This book describes historical events and lives forever changed by someone blessed with the grace to follow a strong desire to be a humble, committed servant to God, country, and family. It's about a life well-lived and remaining forever grateful to serve.

Maj. Frank "Paladin" Cassel
US Army (Retired)

Author's Note

Some names have been changed, or last names omitted, to protect people's identities. The characters are based on real people and the stories on true events. For the sake of a more concise, reader-friendly book, some characters and situations are composites.

The stories revolve around documented historical events. All opinions expressed are solely those of the author and do not reflect any official viewpoints of the United States government. A portion of the proceeds will be donated to charitable and Christian organizations. Thank you for your support.

We know that in all things God works for the good of those who love Him, who have been called according to His purpose.

Drugstore

I didn't want to show any sign of fear that night, though I admit, I was scared. It may have been the first time I seriously feared for my safety, but it wouldn't be the last time. Whenever the doubt and fear start creeping up, I do a simple thing to keep them from taking over. I say a silent prayer: *I'm learning to be content in all things. I can do all things through Christ who strengthens me.*

It was 1992. I was a nineteen-year-old police cadet in Columbus, Georgia. This particular weekend, the vice squad had recruited me to buy alcohol and enter nightclubs underage. This situation was not playing out like any episode of *Miami Vice or 21 Jump Street* that I'd ever seen. I didn't recognize this situation and didn't know what to do. Admittedly, I was new to the job.

My dad was in the army, stationed at Fort Benning for most of his career. I grew up in Columbus and thought I knew the town pretty well. I was a middle-class white kid, the son of a military officer, and had never actually seen the city's underbelly before that night.

I had worked with the same two vice detectives before, Len and Sherry, a man-and-woman team. I enjoyed working with them, but I also knew they only used me to bump up their arrest stats toward the end of the month. They never used me for any of their really important cases, as I'd hoped for. I had actually developed a little bit of a crush on Sherry. It was stupid. She was very open about being gay, not to mention ten years older than me. She was really cool. I liked and respected her a lot and found her physically attractive. Len was married to Sherry's sister, so they did not only work together but were also in-laws.

My job was usually to walk into a store that sold beer, wine, or liquor and attempt to make a purchase. I was nineteen. Everyone

knows a customer has to be at least twenty-one to buy any type of alcohol. Many times, I didn't get carded. If they did card me, I would just pat my pockets and walk out, saying I must have left my wallet in the car.

The evenings I worked these places for vice, we always noticed that the later it got, the less productive we were. It was because the places we busted earlier in the evening started calling around… Then anyone who received a warning would call somebody, and those folks would call other somebodies, and so on. *Hey, vice is out checking. Make sure you're carding people.* Still, working fast, we could end up making ten or twelve misdemeanor arrests during a single shift. This was before smart phones, Internet, or social media. Nowadays information travels faster.

"Furnishing alcohol to a minor" was the charge for anyone who sold to me. The only case I ever felt bad about was one of my first. She was a cute girl who appeared to be in her early twenties. I later found out she was a single mom, working shifts at a local drugstore to support her young daughter. Her ex-boyfriend didn't stick around after he'd gotten her pregnant. She sold me a twelve-pack of Coors Light beer. I felt like a bit of a hypocrite at the time. When I was off-duty, I would often ask one of my friends who actually was of legal age to buy me a twelve-pack of beer. I was in college and ready to party most weekends. Coors Light was my go-to brand.

In my mind, there has always been a dichotomy between what's legally right and what's morally right. Sometimes, those lines blur. It's not always black and white; there's a grey area. There was definitely a double standard going on in my mind that evening. I felt conflicted.

The vice detectives gave me a twenty-dollar-bill and told me to buy whatever I could with it. I walked into the drugstore, stepped over to the walk-in cooler, picked up a twelve-pack of Coors Light, and brought it to the checkout counter. The cute girl working the cash register seemed to be flirting with me. However, I was there to work, so I ignored the flirtation. It was less than twenty bucks for the beer. I handed her the money vice had given me, and she gave me back some change, making sure our hands touched.

I walked outside and had to make a quick decision. Was I going to go through with making this case against her? *I'll be slick and put the beer in my car before Len and Sherry spot me. I'll need to be quick about it.* They were sitting in their detective car, chatting and laughing.

I had some of my own cash on me. I would hand them one of my twenties and tell them the clerk had carded me, so I hadn't bought anything. It would work. I looked over at Len and Sherry's car, and they were stepping out of it. They had already spotted me, so now all I could do was go along with whatever they said.

I didn't want to cause any trouble for the clerk, plus I kind of wanted to keep the beer. The detectives couldn't have cared less about any of that. They were looking to get that misdemeanor arrest. They walked over to me, and Len took the twelve-pack from my hand. "That's the evidence."

Yeah, so let's drink the evidence. I'm thirsty. Sherry was the money custodian, so she asked for the change and receipt. I handed them over reluctantly. I did not want to go back inside the store. Every time I made an alcohol case, I had to go back in with the detectives and point out the person who had sold it to me. I did not want to face the girl again, but knew I would have to. I was following orders, but this one was going to cause me some personal embarrassment. I explained it to Len later, in confidence. He said, with his Southern Georgia twang, "John, it's never personal. It's always just business." *That really doesn't make me feel any better.*

Later, when we went into court, I had to testify against the drugstore clerk. I was dressed in my cadet uniform. I looked different to her because when she sold me the beer, I'd been wearing plain clothes. She was looking down at the floor and crying the entire time we were inside the courtroom. She pleaded "no contest" to the charge. She didn't end up having to serve any jail time. However, she did have to pay a fine. Plus, she'll always have a "furnishing alcohol to a minor" charge on her record.

I couldn't look at her; I felt so bad. When I walked out of the courtroom, she was standing outside, and I heard her say, "I sold you that beer because I liked you, and I thought you were cute." It was

the first time I ever felt like a real jerk. I had to adopt the attitude that if she'd been doing her job properly, she would have checked my ID. It wasn't personal; it was just business.

That still doesn't make me feel any better, but I'm learning to be content in all things.

Yacht Club

One weekend, Len and Sherry sent me into the River City Yacht Club, a fairly well-known gay bar. There I was: a nineteen-year-old straight kid sitting in a gay bar, ordering a beer. This was before pocket-sized cell phones. I had a bag phone, about the size of a cinder block, which stayed in the center console of my '87 Pontiac Firebird. The bag phone had a shoulder strap so I could sling it if I wanted to. *Stylish.* The huge battery lasted about ten minutes if it wasn't plugged in. I never carried that big old bag phone around.

I also had a pager on my belt. Back then, this was as good as it got. If you wanted to get ahold of me, you paged a number to my beeper, and I'd call you back on my car phone when I could get to it. This system was not working for me when I needed to let the detectives know I was ready for them to come in and get me.

In a bar or nightclub scenario, they had to actually walk into the establishment and witness me sitting at the bar with a beer in my hand. I was instructed not to drink it, but just for appearance's sake, I would usually take a few sips anyway. The detectives would watch me from outside just to make sure I got past the person checking IDs at the door. Nine times out of ten, there was either no one working the door or whoever *was* working it wasn't doing a good job of checking. The bartender would usually assume I was twenty-one, or that someone at the door had already checked me, and would serve me whatever I asked for. Len and Sherry would always wait about five minutes before they walked inside, flashing their badges.

I didn't have a real badge, but I wanted one. I had a cadet badge, which looked like something you might get out of a cereal box. I had not been through the academy yet, so I was considered a civilian

employee. I couldn't make an arrest or issue a summons; I had to wait for the detectives to come in and do it. On one occasion, we did have an overzealous cadet declare a citizen's arrest right before vice arrived, but that just looked kind of stupid. He was reprimanded, and they never used him again.

Len and Sherry left me sitting inside the Yacht Club for way longer than normal. I was there for at least twenty minutes before they finally walked in. I know it was twenty minutes because I kept checking my watch. It's funny how twenty minutes can seem like an eternity.

I was, and have been for most of my adult life, of average height at five feet eight inches tall. This one man in the bar was, I estimated, about six foot four. I weighed about 165 pounds. This dude outweighed me by at least a hundred pounds and was built like a linebacker. The worst thing about it, the thing I still remember most to this day, is he was wearing a cowboy outfit like the guy from the Village People.

The place was not very crowded that evening. A couple of guys shot pool at a billiard table and I had to walk past them to get to the bar. A couple of guys stood talking in a corner to my left. There were no women in the place at all. On the big-screen TV in the corner to my right, the comedy program, *In Living Color*, showed skits of Jim Carrey and Jamie Foxx dressed up like women. I loved that show, and it was super funny to me, but not funny at all in this situation.

I have come to refer to the gay cowboy as "Maurice." The place was dimly lit. There was no music playing at all, but when I saw this dude, I immediately thought of the lyrics to the Steve Miller song, "The Joker." "Some people call me the space cowboy (yeah). Some call me the gangster of love. Some people call me Maurice (whaa whaa). 'Cause I speak of the pompitous of love."

Maybe because it was a slow night; they didn't want to pay someone to check IDs at the door. I walked in and went straight to the bar. The bartender should have recognized I was underage, or questionable at least. He must have known no one was working the door. He should have carded me, but he didn't. I ordered a Coors Light, so he brought over a twelve-ounce can and set it down in front

of me. The way my mind works, I'm always contingency planning: *If this happens, I'm gonna do that. If that happens, I'm gonna do this.* It's a big part of what has kept me alive to this day, I believe. Contingency planning and the grace of God are major components of what I call a "survival mindset." They help me stay prepared for whatever life may throw at me.

I assumed that I was the only straight person in the Yacht Club, based on the place's reputation. I scoped out the scene upon walking in and deliberately sat down at the opposite end of the bar from the big dude wearing the cowboy outfit. I expected to be there no more than five minutes and didn't want to cause any trouble.

Out of the corner of my eye, I noticed Maurice staring at me. He scooted over about three barstools in my direction. There were still at least ten barstools between us, but the space seemed to close quickly. I pretended to watch *In Living Color.* I checked my watch, sipped my beer, and kept waiting for vice to arrive. *Any minute now. Any second.*

About six more minutes passed before Maurice moved over again, three more barstools in my direction. I could tell he was moving slowly and was stumbling a little. I looked at his drink: *maybe a Jack and Coke.* My hope was that he'd consumed about ten of those before I got there. With any luck, he was off balance so I could knock him down if necessary. At this point, it was clear he was moving closer. I asked the bartender for a beer mug, so he brought one over. If I needed a makeshift weapon, I'd rather have a heavy glass mug in my hand than a twelve-ounce aluminum can.

As Maurice moved a few more barstools closer, I gripped my mug by the handle. Where was vice? It had been about fifteen minutes. Had they gotten distracted or been called away? Had they forgotten about me? Were they just messing with me? *Maybe I should just get up and walk out. I don't want to mess this up.*

I'm diplomatic, not violent, by nature. My first inclination was to politely tell Maurice I wasn't interested, then get up and walk away. However, judging from his physical appearance, drunken mannerisms, and the way he glared at me, I considered the possibility that

he might not take it well. He was two barstools away when Len and Sherry finally walked in. *Oh, thank Jesus.*

The lights came on, and *In Living Color* was turned off. Badges got flashed, and Maurice disappeared into the restroom. The bartender was charged with "allowing a minor to enter a nightclub" as well as "furnishing alcohol to a minor."

In most cases, the accused parties were not physically arrested. Usually, they would receive a summons to appear in court, the same as if they were being issued a traffic citation. The only time anyone was ever actually arrested was if they showed some kind of attitude or acted like a jerk. *Being nice and still being nice, until it's time not to be nice, goes a long way.* In this case, the bartender received a summons. Len and Sherry got their two arrest stats.

They later admitted that they'd left me in the bar longer than usual, on purpose. I didn't come right out and ask them; they could just tell I was annoyed. They had a good laugh and said it was just to see how I would handle the situation. After they admitted it, I laughed too. I told them about Maurice the Space Cowboy making his way toward me and about how I was getting ready to smash my beer mug over his head.

"I'll go out fighting," I said. We were back at the vice office, so they could type up their reports for the evening. I tried talking loud and tough so the other vice detectives could hear me. They didn't seem too impressed. I'm sure they'd seen plenty of young punks talking a good game with not much to back it up.

The vice office was located inside an old church building in downtown Columbus, which I found really cool because it reminded me of episodes of *21 Jump Street*. I thought I'd be working undercover like Tom Hanson, Johnny Depp's character. I liked hanging out at the old church with the vice detectives, but they kept strange hours, so I didn't get to hang out there often. Their shift went from about six in the evening until two in the morning, plus overtime if needed. I wanted to be a vice detective. *You have to start somewhere. You're just paying your dues now.* That's what I kept telling myself, but that aspiration never worked out for me. I was naïve about the "good old boy network" at the Columbus Police Department (CPD). Only over the

course of the ten years I spent as a cadet and patrolman there would it become apparent. I was definitely not one of the good old boys.

Be still before the Lord and wait patiently for Him.

Nightclubs

As a teen growing up in the eighties, I watched way too many cop shows on television. I was in my senior year at Hardaway High School in 1990 and had already been accepted into the criminal justice program at Columbus State University. It was the only degree program that really even interested me. I thought maybe if I had a bachelor's degree in criminal justice, I could apply to become an FBI agent, especially if I had some local law enforcement experience under my belt.

I was enrolled in Army ROTC throughout high school as an elective and enjoyed it. However, I never got the sense that a career in the military would be a good fit for me. I wanted to be a street cop. My dad, having spent a career in the army himself, even discouraged me from joining the military. He wanted me to stay home and attend the local college. I talked with my ROTC instructor, Sergeant Frost, and he's the one who encouraged me to put in an application for Columbus PD's cadet program.

Sergeant Frost told me how, in the early eighties, CPD had planted a police cadet at Hardaway. The cadet had graduated from a different high school two years prior, but no one at Hardaway knew him. He "transferred in" about the middle of the school year. Over the next few months, he made friends with the kids known to use and deal drugs. By the end of the school year, this cadet had apparently busted up a very large drug ring at Hardaway. I was sold. That was what I wanted to do. I drove downtown to pick up an application the same day.

After the Yacht Club bust, Len and Sherry rewarded me for a job well done by sending me into a few of the local strip clubs. The one I recall specifically was called Satin Sheets Lounge. It was

a gentlemen's club, located downtown on Broadway. It's not there anymore, but it stands out in my mind because it was kind of nice.

The soldiers stationed at Fort Benning referred to Victory Drive as "VD Drive." Most of the bars and strip clubs along it were cheap and trashy but were close to the base. They catered to young GIs on weekend liberty, most of whom would not venture all the way downtown to visit a classier place like Satin Sheets. *Hey vice, this place is kinda nice. You can leave me in here for thirty or forty minutes.* They left me there for the standard five minutes, of course.

Vice used me for these assignments mostly when I was nineteen. I hired on at the department at eighteen, but I think I was too new for them to trust me during my first year. After I turned twenty, they stopped using me and started using younger cadets. It was kind of an unwritten rule. By the time a person turned twenty, the shock factor in court was gone: "You served this nineteen-year-old kid alcohol? Shame on you." As opposed to: "You served this twenty-year-old guy alcohol?"

I was still hoping they'd put me undercover at a local high school. One weekend they used me as well as two fellow cadets, Jim and Reggie, to enter a couple of the more popular dance clubs: Big Al's Place and the Choctaw.

Jim, Reggie, and I had become good friends and hung around together many weekends even when we were off-duty. It seemed natural for us to work as a buddy team to go into these places together. We had a great time that weekend. We were young, hanging out, and getting into these nightclubs underage. *Look at us. We're ordering cocktails, having a few laughs, and getting paid to do it.*

Jim's go-to drink was 7 and 7. Reggie was a gin and tonic man. I stepped it up a notch from beer and had started ordering tequila sunrises. By the end of the evening, vice was able to rack up multiple charges on these places for allowing three teenage boys to get inside and order alcohol.

Columbus, Georgia, is a military town. When the soldiers from Fort Benning get a weekend pass, it's common to see groups of them walking around together, visiting bars and clubs. Jim, Reggie, and I were young and clean-cut, so I guess the people working at these

clubs assumed we were GIs on a weekend pass. My tolerance for alcohol was really low. It only took a few sips from a tequila sunrise for me to feel a little tipsy, so I had to pace myself. I didn't want anyone to have to drive me home at the end of the night. Jim and Reggie stopped being used for these busts shortly after this because they turned twenty.

There are exceptions to every rule, even the unwritten ones. There was a pretty female cadet named Pam. Vice would dress her up to resemble a prostitute and pose her out on Victory Drive. All she had to do was stand there, and the cases would come to her. Detectives would sit where they could keep an eye on her and then wait for guys to roll up in cars, offering Pam a ride. She was told never to get into the cars and not to suggest sex or money. The guys had to suggest it first. Otherwise, it could be considered entrapment. She was so productive on those weekends, and vice racked up so many pandering and solicitation charges that they used her for the whole three years she was a cadet.

Watch over us, Lord, as we seek to do your work. For you are a shield around me. You are my glory, the one who holds my head high.

Rock House

The Rock House was one of the last places I would work for vice because I was getting ready to turn twenty in October. It was still warm outside during the day but starting to get cool in the evenings. I remember wearing my favorite light jacket and blue jeans. I checked myself in the mirror before I headed out: *I could pass for mid-twenties.* Now when I look at pictures of myself from back then: *No way! I looked like a fifteen-year-old kid! How did I not get carded?*

During the Rock House bust, Sherry and I were supposed to pose as girlfriend and boyfriend. I was fairly sure though, even back then, a nineteen-year-old kid walking in with a thirtyish-year-old woman didn't look quite right.

She drove us there in a beat-up red GMC pickup truck, a city motor pool vehicle vice used to make drug buys sometimes. It looked like a hundred other old, beat-up pickup trucks in Columbus. The plan was Sherry and I would arrive at the bar around seven o'clock and stay for about three hours. The rest of the squad would hang back and then show up around ten to bust the place. This would give Sherry plenty of time to try scoring some cocaine.

The Rock House, just outside the gates of Fort Benning on South Lumpkin Road, attracted many young soldiers on weekend liberty leave. The club advertised live heavy metal bands and cheap booze. Bikers hung out there too. Fights, cuttings, stabbings, and shootings were common occurrences. The place also had a reputation for admitting underage people and allowing illegal substances to be sold on the premises. My job would be to enter the club, then sit there and order cocktails for Sherry and myself. Her job would be to make a dope buy. This was different from anything I had worked

before, so I was excited. I felt like I was being trusted and moving up the ladder.

There was a guy working the door that evening, checking IDs. Sherry and I were holding hands as if on a date. She said something to the guy, but I'm still not sure to this day what it was. She carried herself with such confidence and walked in there like she owned the place. I admired that. The door guy waved us through.

I was inside, so that was one charge right there. We sat at a small table not far from the main stage. I almost felt as if I was on a real date. A heavy metal cover band was playing on stage. The waitress came for our drink order, and we had to shout over the music. I asked Sherry what she felt like drinking, and she replied with, "Whatever you're having." I could tell she was scoping the place out, looking for someone to buy drugs from. She had also spotted a young-looking GI sitting at the bar, so this would be an additional charge if he was underage. It turned out he was, in fact, an eighteen-year-old soldier from Fort Benning. He was going through basic training and had managed to sneak off the base.

Generally speaking, whenever a soldier from Benning got caught up in something dumb like this, they received fair treatment from our PD. I believe any soldier who has spent time at Benning, or around Columbus, would agree with that statement. We would normally notify their drill sergeant or commanding officer who would meet us at the main gate of the base. We would hand the soldier over to their superior officer and let them handle it from there. It usually resulted in some type of administrative military punishment instead of civilian legal action.

I told the waitress, "Two tequila sunrises." Actually I shouted it to her so she could hear me. I must have sustained some partial hearing loss in that place; the music was so loud. I knew we would be there for at least three hours. Why I chose to start off with a tequila drink, I have no idea. *Liquor before beer, you're in the clear. Beer before liquor, never been sicker. I'm still not sure how that saying came about or if it's even true. I'll order beers on the next round.*

We drank our tequila sunrises within minutes. I ordered another round of the same, like an idiot. Sherry was drinking fast, and I

was trying to keep up. You know how when you're sitting down and drinking, you don't realize how tipsy you are until you go to stand up? We drank the second round, and I half expected her to have to use the ladies' room by then, but she didn't. I stood up to walk to the men's room after my second cocktail and realized I was a bit wobbly on my feet. I took care of my business and walked back to our table. I think Sherry could tell I was a little tipsy, though she showed no sign of slowing down. If the city was paying for her to have drinks for three hours, she was going to enjoy it. She had ordered another tequila sunrise for herself and a Coors Light for me.

I sat down next to her and scooted a little closer, as if we were really on a date. I put my arm around her. I was getting a little too comfortable. She leaned toward me to tell me something, but I thought she was leaning in to kiss me. I had my right arm around her, so she took her left hand and ran it up the back of my neck and through my hair. I got chills. She leaned toward my right ear to tell me something. I could feel her nose and lips against my ear. I could hear her say, "Hey, remember, we're working here. This is all good for show, but I'm gonna get up and go to the ladies' room." I nodded my head to let her know I understood.

Reality started to set in. We were going to be in this biker bar for at least another two hours. I was an underage kid, unarmed and slightly intoxicated. I still do not know to this day whether or not Sherry was packing. I had my arm around her waist a couple of times and didn't feel a gun there. She wasn't carrying a purse. She may have had a small gun tucked into one of her boots. I'm honestly not sure. I started contingency planning again.

She got up and walked to the ladies' room, and I started to nurse my beer. I took a deep breath to slow my heart rate. *We're working here.* I needed that reality check. I watched another woman follow her into the restroom. A short while later, Sherry came out and sat back down next to me. The whole bust got cut short, so I guess she must have had a direct communication line to the rest of the squad. Maybe she was wearing a wire. All I know for sure is I was not expecting vice to show up until around ten o'clock. Sherry leaned

against me and said, "I scored some coke in the bathroom." I nodded my head again.

Lights came on in the club, and the music came to a screeching halt around half past eight, much earlier than I expected. *It's okay. We've got everything we need to make some good cases. There may even be time to go bust another place.*

"Allowing a minor to enter a nightclub," two counts, was charged to the gentleman who was supposed to have been checking IDs at the door. One charge was for letting me in, and the other was for letting in the underage GI. Someone would have to take the eighteen-year-old soldier back to the base. Technically, he could have been charged with "minor in possession of alcohol," but they just called his drill sergeant to pick him up.

"Furnishing alcohol to a minor" was the charge for the bartender, as well as for our waitress. This part doesn't seem particularly fair, I know. They just assumed the guy working the door had checked my ID on the way in.

"Sale of a schedule-two narcotic," a felony charge, was for the woman who sold the dime bag of coke to Sherry in the ladies' room. It was a productive night, and it was still early.

Vice detectives walked around the whole bar, going from person to person, checking IDs. They even checked the place's liquor license. When they came around to me, I had my driver's license in hand. I looked up to see which detective was approaching me. It was Len. I gave him a tipsy smile and handed him my ID. He acted as if he was really studying it, then handed it back to me and just said, "Okay," acting as if I was of legal age.

Ha ha, I love this.

Sherry and I were allowed to leave, so she drove us back to the vice office. I wasn't sure if I'd be sober enough to drive my personal car home. I had consumed two tequila cocktails, which seemed to be fairly strong pours. I could really taste the tequila. I also had two beers, all within about an hour and a half. It was a lot for me in a short period of time. When we returned to the vice office, the lieutenant wanted to get me out of there before any of the people who were charged started coming through for processing.

"Hey, John. You okay to drive home?"

I didn't speak, just nodded. I think he could tell I was not okay. He looked at Sherry with a disappointed dad expression, like, "You got this kid drunk, and now we have to call a squad car to take him home." Sherry just shrugged it off.

A patrol car picked me up from the vice office and drove me home. I called the next morning, and they took me back for my car. It didn't cost me a thing, except maybe an ounce of pride. Sherry had consumed more alcohol than I had, and she was still sober as a judge.

Just because of the way things worked out, Sherry and I never worked together again. I would see her in passing around headquarters or in court, and we would say hi. Things seemed somewhat awkward between us. Maybe it was just my perception. Shortly afterward, she moved up to the Metro Narcotics Task Force, which had federal jurisdiction. She was sworn in as a federal agent. I heard that eventually she went to work for the DEA in Atlanta.

The righteous shall live by faith and do the work of God.

Academy Appointment

During my downtime, I would borrow a McGruff the Crime Dog costume from the community relations office. I'd go around visiting local elementary schools with a school resource officer who would talk to the kids about "taking a bite out of crime." Then I'd come out to give hugs and shake hands dressed up as McGruff.

I worked a few more small-time alcohol cases for Len and his new partner, a detective named Rick, but then I turned twenty, and vice stopped using me. The personnel office assigned me to the auto theft squad. I liked working with the auto theft detectives, and they let me wear plain clothes. They didn't make me wear my cadet uniform like when I worked the front desk at headquarters. I was content for the time being. It was a lot of mundane administrative work though. *This is the way police work is, I guess. It's 90 percent sheer boredom, 7 percent excitement, and 3 percent fear. You'll have to learn to escalate and de-escalate; to ramp up and ramp down.*

As the auto theft cadet, my primary job was to drive over to the impound lot on Brennan Road and write down the VIN and license plate numbers of all the cars that had been towed the previous evening. Then I'd return to the office and run the numbers through GCIS (Georgia Criminal Information System) to see if any came back stolen. I got about two "hits" a day on average but couldn't do anything except notify one of the detectives. I felt like a glorified secretary. I did that for about eight months. One day in June of 1993, I got called into the personnel office. I thought I'd done something wrong.

Lieutenant Jack sat me down and asked if I planned to take any college classes over the summer. I didn't know where he was

going with this conversation. I had finished my associate's degree but planned to keep chipping away at a bachelor's. He knew that.

"Actually, I was thinking about taking the summer quarter off, sir. I could use a break. I'll start back in the fall," I told him.

"Good. I was hoping you'd say that," he replied. "I have a slot open in the July academy. You'll start your training next month."

I was so excited; I didn't know what to say. I finally said, "But, LT, I'm only twenty. I won't be twenty-one until October."

Columbus PD's policy had always been that you had to be twenty-one before they'd swear you in, but they were about to make an exception.

"I know when your birthday is," he said. "I talked to the captain about you, and he's already signed off on it. The state academy is two-months long, and the city in-service academy is another month. You'll be twenty-one by the time you hit the street with a training officer. You've been with us for over two years, and you've done a good job. You'll attend the July academy…unless you'd rather keep waiting."

Wow! I really did not know what to say or do other than shake his hand and thank him. It seems like I said, "I won't let you down, LT," or something to that effect.

For I know the plans I have for you declares the Lord, to give you a future and a hope.

Shooting at Big Al's Place

"It's all over now but the cryin'." That's what my good friend Ron used to say. He was an auto theft detective when I worked there as a cadet. I was twenty; he was forty-four. Ron was the same age as my dad at the time and the age I am now as I write this. I've always looked up to my dad and have a ton of respect and admiration for him. He's a Vietnam vet and retired Airborne Ranger officer. You can't mess with that, but it wasn't what I wanted to be. I wanted to be a cop.

Ron was also a Vietnam vet. However, he'd gotten out of the military after the war and joined Columbus PD. He had been a vice detective for a number of years but, for one reason or another, was now in auto theft. Okay, I know the reason. He told me the story once.

The nightclub I mentioned earlier, Big Al's Place, along with several other clubs in town, kept getting broken into. The perpetrator would sneak in through the air ducts in the roof, bypass the alarm system, and steal any cash he could find in the office. It seemed like one person doing it based on the evidence and MO (modus operandi).

Big Al hired Ron to sit in the club overnight and keep watch. It should have been easy money. Sure enough, one morning at around three, as he sat there reading a book, Ron heard some noises coming from overhead.

The suspect made his way down from the roof, through the air duct, and into the club. He dropped down very close to the office where Ron was, as if familiar with the place. Ron drew his pistol. "Hey! Police! Don't you move!"

The perp bolted for the front door. *It's all over now but the cryin'.* The front door was only locked from the outside, so the suspect easily pushed his way out. Ron gave chase. The guy was dressed like a ninja in a black hoodie, black jeans, and black tennis shoes. He ran like a track star. He was faster and more agile than Ron, but Ron was doing his best to keep the dude in sight.

Ron had his walkie-talkie in his left hand, but that big old radio was as heavy as a brick. His pistol was in his right hand. He chased the suspect east through the wooded area on the other side of Armour Road. Ron was wearing a blue police raid jacket, blue jeans, and black boots. It was important for him to communicate that he was in plain clothes so as to avoid any "blue on blue" friendly fire. He was doing his best to give his description, location, and direction of travel over the air so the backup units could get to him, but he inadvertently dropped his radio. Ron was out of breath but kept chasing the suspect.

The perp kept turning around to look at Ron, and he had something shiny in his right hand. Ron thought it might have been a weapon but couldn't be sure. It was dark outside, but the moonlight and streetlights reflected off the shiny object. Ron had taken off running in such a hurry that he'd left his flashlight on the desk back at the office.

Bang! Ron let one shot from his pistol ring out, which tore into the guy's right leg. It slowed the suspect down, but he kept running. Ron was firing the standard-issued vice detective Smith & Wesson 9mm semiautomatic pistol. The rest of the department still carried Smith & Wesson .357 magnum revolvers. Vice detectives carried those pistols because they were smaller, lighter, more concealable, and held more rounds. Another advantage for Ron was that his pistol was equipped with tritium night sights, which made it easier to get a good sight picture in low-light conditions.

The perp turned around to see how close Ron was. What was the shiny object in his hand? A gun? A knife? *Bang!* Ron let another one rip. It tore through the guy's left leg this time, but he kept running. *What is this dude, the Energizer bunny? He just keeps going and going.* The adrenaline was pumping for both of them.

Ron stopped running and raised his pistol, aiming the sights at the suspect's center mass, as police are trained to do. It was dark outside, but the light from the full moon made it easy enough for Ron to make out the perp's silhouette. Ron was breathing hard from running, so his sights kept rising and falling. *He's getting away!*

Ron took a deep breath and held it. *Steady. Squeeze.* He saw light reflect off the shiny object again. *Bang!* This one nicked the suspect's lower spinal cord. Not exactly center mass but good enough to finally end the chase. The guy dropped to the ground like a sack of potatoes. It was an effective shot from about forty yards away in the dark.

After Ron told me this story, I started going out to the shooting range and practicing on an average-size human silhouette target from forty yards away in low-light conditions. I did it using only the night sights on my pistol, no flashlight. I also did it after running a quarter mile as fast as I could, so I was breathing hard. It's not easy, but as with anything else, the more you practice, the better you get. I've learned over the years, you train for the conditions you might actually find yourself fighting in. If you only practice and train under ideal conditions, you'll freeze up in an actual life-or-death situation.

"Don't you move!" Ron yelled as he approached with his gun still drawn. The perp was lying on the ground facedown. Ron was watching for any movement but mostly watched the suspect's hands. Every cop knows that if someone is going to hurt or kill you, it's most likely going to be with their hands. The guy wasn't moving, other than breathing hard, and his hands were empty. *He did have something, I'm sure of it. He must have dropped it somewhere or tossed it. I gotta find it.*

Blue lights and sirens were approaching now from every direction but still off in the distance. Every police unit on that side of the city was responding to his initial radio call. Ron was securing the suspect's hands with cuffs as he saw several officers with flashlights running through the woods.

"Over here!" he called out.

As the officers got closer, Ron held up his badge with his left hand. He still had his pistol in his right hand, covering the suspect.

His eyes searched the ground for the shiny object. *Nothing. Did I imagine it?*

"Give me a flashlight!" Ron called out to an approaching officer. "And watch him until the ambulance gets here!"

One of the officers handed Ron a flashlight and stayed with the suspect as Ron and the other officers searched the ground in the surrounding area. "Got it!" one of the uniforms called out. The perp had tossed it about thirty feet to his right, just before he fell. It was a little chrome-plated .380 pistol. It was a cheap piece of junk, what we would call a "Saturday night special," yet it could still be deadly if used effectively. The suspect had stolen it from the office of one of the other nightclubs he'd burglarized. There were rounds in the magazine, and the safety was off. However, there was no round in the chamber. Ron figured the guy was turning around and pointing the .380 at him while they were running. He'd probably even pulled the trigger. Being unskilled with guns, the suspect had never racked a round into the chamber, so the gun just went *click* instead of *bang*.

As it turned out, the guy was a former Big Al's manager who had been fired for pocketing cash from the office. He lived after Ron shot him, but he never walked again. He was confined to a wheelchair for the rest of his life. He also had to go away to prison for a couple years after being convicted of the nightclub burglaries and weapon charges.

All who came before me were thieves and robbers.

The Dude

Ron was placed on administrative paid leave immediately following the shooting. I asked him how he felt then because some cops find admin leave demeaning. The department takes your badge and gun away while internal affairs investigates. Many officers are made to feel as though they did something wrong, even if they did everything right. The department makes you talk to a shrink to determine whether you're experiencing any post-traumatic stress.

Ron took it all in stride. "I treated it like a paid vacation and went to the beach. What else was I gonna do?" That was his nature. He was one of the most laid-back, friendly, and funny people I've ever known…until it was time to take care of business. He could flip a switch and go from zero to a hundred. It's how I wanted to be.

Just to be funny and kind of a smart aleck, Ron would wear a Hawaiian shirt for court appearances when he worked in vice. Department regulation was if you weren't wearing the standard-issued uniform, you had to wear a coat and tie for court appearances. During my earlier days as a cadet, I had seen him in court wearing blue jeans and a Hawaiian shirt, with a coat and tie. He was technically within regulation, but he sure annoyed a judge and a few supervisors with that. *This guy thinks he's Sonny Crockett and Thomas Magnum rolled into one.*

Ron's actions during the shooting were deemed justified, and he returned to duty. However, he was taken out of vice and placed in auto theft. I only asked him once if that was his choice or the department's. He never would tell me. He just said, "It's an answer I'll take to my grave, bud." And he did.

Ron passed away of a sudden massive heart attack in May of 2012. I was working in Iraq when I got the news. I had just seen him one month earlier. My family and I had driven from Virginia to Georgia to visit with family and friends during my kids' spring break. Ron and I had e-mailed back and forth a few times but had not seen each other in person for almost ten years. I got caught up in my overseas deployments after 9/11 and pushed many of my friends aside. *I'm too busy; I don't have time.* Now I have regrets about it.

Ron used to do and say some of the funniest things I've ever seen or heard. I call them "Ronisms" and started remembering some of them while writing this book.

There was a sergeant in auto theft notorious for letting out silent farts in the car with the windows rolled up. They were some of the worst you could imagine, and you wouldn't even know it was happening until the odor started assaulting your nostrils. Once, they let me ride with them to serve a search warrant. Ron was driving, the sarge was riding up front, and I was sitting in back. Sarge let one of those nasty farts loose, and Ron yelled, "Hot almighty, Sarge! That's bad enough to knock a buzzard off a gut wagon! That's bad enough to make a freight train take a dirt road!"

Between rolling down my window, trying not to inhale the flatulent air, and laughing at Ron, I couldn't breathe. I thought I'd pass out but was able to finally get a breath of fresh air, calm down, and eventually regain my composure.

We were serving the search warrant at an auto salvage yard on Morris Road. Word on the street was that the owner was running an illegal "chop shop" operation, so we expected to find some stolen cars on the premises. The business owner was working in the front office that day. I noticed he was in a wheelchair. The sarge showed him the search warrant, but the guy would not take his eyes off Ron.

He started shaking and turned as white as a ghost. I looked at Ron who acted as if he didn't know the dude. I had a feeling it was the guy from the Big Al's shooting. I couldn't believe he was out on parole already. He was the only one working at the salvage yard that day, and we did find several stolen cars on the property, so he was charged with more felonies to add to his record. I guess he'd

graduated from burglarizing businesses to receiving stolen property. Come to find out, although he had to serve some prison time, he also received a monetary settlement from the city because of the shooting. He'd used the money to buy this salvage yard. *That's messed up. He shouldn't have received any kind of settlement. He pointed a gun at a cop. He's lucky to still be alive.*

We had the stolen cars towed to the police impound lot and made the guy close down his business for the day. We called for a patrol unit to transport him to the county jail. After the suspect was gone, Ron looked at me and smiled. "That's the guy I shot. I didn't think I'd ever see him again. I can't believe he's out on parole already."

"I was thinking the same thing," I replied. "But it's a small world. You must have known you might run into him again somewhere, sometime." I still find it a surprisingly wise thing for me to have said. I was young and dumb. Okay, not dumb. We'll say "still learning."

"I reckon," Ron said. "When he saw me, he started shaking like a possum pooping persimmon seeds."

I just laughed. *Another Ronism.*

Something was nagging at me in April of 2012, telling me I needed to go see my buddy, Ron. I was getting ready to deploy overseas again and knew he was working as a training instructor at the police academy in Columbus. I showed up one day and surprised him. He was so happy to see me and gave me a great big bear hug. My son was fourteen, and I took him with me so that Ron could see how big he'd gotten. Ron had not seen Nick since he was four.

I gave Ron a challenge coin from the team I was serving with because I knew he kept a collection of them. The identifying information on the coin was vague, so he asked which organization it was from. I didn't say anything, just handed him my badge and credentials. He took a look and said, "Ha ha! Look at that! I always knew you had it in you!" with a great big proud smile. He studied the badge and creds for a minute, then handed them back. We shook hands, hugged, and parted ways. We promised to get together for beer and wings after I returned from my deployment. It would never happen, but I'm so glad I went to see him that day at the academy.

If something inside you tells you to go see someone, don't ignore it. You never know whether you'll get another chance. It's another thing I've come to learn over the years.

I was back in Iraq a month later and was on my laptop in the team room, getting ready to Skype with Kim and the kids. I went onto Facebook to remind Ron about getting together for beer and wings when I returned to the States. I saw "Rest in Peace" posts on his page and sat there in disbelief for several minutes. My old friend was gone. He was sixty-two and close to retiring. *What happened?*

I called Jim on his cell phone to find out. Apparently, Ron had made a morning court appearance, then went home to change clothes and eat lunch around noon. He'd parked in the garage and entered his house through the utility room. That's where his daughter found him when she got home from school. He'd suffered a major cardiac arrest.

Thank you, God, for giving me a friend and mentor like Ron. You shall wipe away every tear from their eyes. There will be no more death or mourning or crying or pain.

Foot Chase

"**M**an, I'm tired! I'm tired of chasing you! If you don't come out from under this house by the count of ten! Well, let's just say I've got my gun in my hand! I'm gonna start busting caps under this house at random! Wherever they hit, they hit!"

I actually said that to a suspect once. He made me so mad. I know there's no excuse for talking to any citizen like that, but this guy really made me lose my cool.

I had received a 911 call to Peabody Apartments, a government housing project. I got called there often because it was on my assigned beat: beat twelve. The caller was being physically abused by her boyfriend and had taken about as much as she could stand.

Many low-income housing tenants are single moms. When they sign the lease for government housing, they agree not to let a man move into their apartment. However, many tenants ignore this stipulation. There are plenty of freeloading men ready and willing to take advantage.

I responded to the call. I was a one-man unit that night, and there was no one available to back me up.

"Headquarters to three-twelve."

That was me: I was three-twelve. "Go ahead, headquarters."

"Eighty-two hundred at Peabody Apartments." *Eighty-two hundred. Another domestic disturbance call.* I rolled my eyes but advised the dispatcher that I was en route.

When I showed up, the subject who had been beating up on his girlfriend took off running. I chased after him, but my body armor and all the gear around my waist slowed me down. He was faster than I was. I chased him for about three blocks into the old Jordan-

Johnson neighborhood. He rounded a corner, and I lost sight of him. I rounded the same corner with my gun drawn. *You never know if you're going to round a corner and get ambushed.* I didn't see him. *There's no way he just disappeared like that. No way.*

I stopped running. It was hot that evening, at least ninety degrees, and I was sweating through my uniform. Columbus, Georgia, sits in a valley and has this way of holding in heat, like soup in a bowl. The air was thick and humid around me, and my body armor clung to me.

The old house I was standing next to had a crawlspace under it, so I had a gut feeling the punk had ducked under it. It was just starting to get dark outside. I pointed my flashlight and gun under there but didn't see anything except rusty pipes and foundation work. I still had a hunch he was under there, but there was no way I was crawling after him. My Smith & Wesson 4586 semiautomatic pistol had a round in the chamber.

By this time, most of the department had transitioned from the old .357 revolvers to the new .45 pistols. My academy class was the first to graduate with pistols. We carried our service pistols with a round in the chamber; it was SOP. (standard operating procedure). I racked the slide on my pistol just for sound effects. *Click-clack.* Later on, I had to look around on the ground and retrieve the live round that ejected from the chamber. I stuck it into my pocket and topped off my magazine with it later, when I was by myself. Not a great tactical practice to rack a live round out of the chamber, but in this case, I considered the racking sound necessary to help coax the subject out from under the house.

When I went to the police academy, my goal was to be top shooter as well as honor graduate. I ended up getting one out of two. I got the honor graduate award but was beaten out of the top shooter spot by a fire department arson investigator from LaGrange named Romero. It was only by a couple of points, but it's always bothered me. I think I could beat him now if we were to go back to the range together. *Consider this a friendly challenge if you're reading, Romero.*

In a stressful situation, all you have to do is remember the basics, even if the stressful situation is someone shooting back at you.

Grip, sight picture, front sight focus, trigger control, *press...press...press...bang!* Shooting accurately is kind of like taking a picture with a camera. My dad taught me that when he taught me how to shoot, way back when. You take a snapshot in time of where you want your bullet to go, and that's where it will go. People sometimes use the phrase "pull the trigger," but it's actually more of a press, like pressing a button with your fingertip.

"Fast is fine, but accuracy is everything. In a gunfight, you need to take your time in a hurry." Wyatt Earp said that.

I was not really going to shoot under the house, or at this guy, unless he presented an actual threat, but he thought I was based on my demeanor, language, and the sound effects from my pistol.

"Okay, sir, I'm coming out. Don't shoot. I'm showing you my hands," I heard him say from underneath the house.

"Well, get out here then! I'm still counting!"

I could see him start to emerge from behind a piece of foundation work in the crawlspace. He was crouching and had his hands out in front of him. His hands were empty.

At the police academy, they teach you the basics and give you a good foundation to build on. However, once you get out on the street you quickly realize things are different from what they taught you in school. Things happen fast in real life, and you have to use your best judgment to make split-second decisions. Hopefully, you make the right ones. I called out my location over the radio. Because I'd been involved in a foot chase, every other cop in my section dropped whatever call they were on and started heading toward my location. Code two; that's what we called running with lights and siren. I could hear the sirens.

"Slow it down," I said over the radio. "All units, you can slow it down." The sirens quieted. You don't want emergency responders running code two any longer than necessary. It's a risk to civilian drivers and pedestrians.

Jim was almost always the first one to back me up on calls. We looked out for each other on the street. The suspect had low-crawled the rest of the way out from under the house. I still had the guy at gunpoint, in case he reached for his pockets or waistband. He

cooperated and lay facedown on the ground with his hands behind his head, fingers interlaced. Jim came running up, cuffs already positioned in his right hand.

Jim could apply the "speed cuffing" technique faster than anyone else in our squad. You use the suspect's wrists as leverage and push the cuffs against the wrists rapidly so the ratchets spin around and lock in place. Before I knew it, the subject was cuffed up and sitting in the back of Jim's car. Jim transported us back to where my car was so that I could take the girlfriend's statement. She was adamant about pressing charges, so I moved her boyfriend from Jim's car over to mine for transport. The victim had some visible injuries, but she refused medical treatment, so I gave her a witness summons to appear in court the next day.

I left Jim's cuffs on the suspect and gave Jim a set of mine. He and I each carried two sets of handcuffs because we worked in a busy area where we made a lot of arrests. Sometimes you needed two sets anyway, if you had to arrest someone large. You had to hook two sets together, because their hands could not physically get close enough together for a single set to work. It just made sense to carry two sets. Hands always get cuffed behind a person's back, by the way, for officer safety. You never want to cuff a suspect's hands in front of them out of comfort or convenience. I'll tell another story about that later.

Two is one, and one is none. I carried two of almost every piece of critical gear. Two sets of handcuffs. Two guns. Two flashlights. Two radio batteries. Two pocket knives. The mentality here is to always think your primary might malfunction or get damaged, rendering it useless, so you might have to go to your secondary. My primary sidearm was the department-issued full-sized .45 semiautomatic, but my backup gun was a little .38 snub-nose revolver I carried in an ankle holster. My primary flashlight was the big department-issued Maglite, but my backup was a Mini Mag I carried in a pocket. You always want to train and be proficient with your backup gear just as you do with your primary gear.

I took the guy to the county jail and charged him with "simple battery" for beating up his girlfriend. I also charged him with the catch-all city ordinance "disorderly conduct" for running away from

me and hiding under the house. Technically, I could have charged him with "obstruction," but didn't. I figured I had traumatized him enough by threatening to shoot underneath the house.

When we went into court the next day, the girlfriend showed up and wanted to drop the charges. I wasn't surprised, as that happened more times than not. *At least she showed up. A lot of times, they don't even bother to show up.*

Because he was living in her apartment, even though he was not supposed to be, I'd charged him under the domestic violence act. She was not supposed to be able to drop the charges. However, it was always left to the judge's discretion.

On these domestic cases, many times, the girlfriend would feel bad the next day for calling the police on her man and would ask for the charges to be dropped. The city court judge knew that if he sent the charges up to the next level, the state judge would usually reduce or dismiss them altogether, if the girlfriend did not want to testify. In this case, the city judge allowed the "simple battery" to be dismissed. However, because I had to chase the suspect and he hid underneath that old house, the "disorderly conduct" stuck. The guy spent thirty days in jail and had to pay a small fine.

I never got called back to that same apartment again, and I hope it's because she decided to remove that man from her life.

Killing Maggie May

Domestic violence is a vicious cycle, and it escalates over time. It doesn't get better or go away. The abusive person is usually an abuser for life. He or she might be able to hide their abusive, manipulative behavior temporarily, but eventually, the downward spiral begins again. One day, the person may be charming and pleasant, but the next day, they turn cruel and hateful again. Things might seem to get better for a while, but they eventually get worse again. My next story is just one of many real-world examples I can give you.

"Headquarters to three-twelve," the call came over the radio. I had just sat down at Hardee's to eat a burger. *This is usually how it goes.*

"Go ahead, headquarters."

"Eighty-two-hundred at 307 Twenty-Eighth Street," the dispatcher said. She was giving me the run code and address for a domestic disturbance.

I acknowledged that I was en route to the call. I was familiar with the address; we got called there at least twice a month. *George and Maggie are at it again.* Usually, it was George beating up on Maggie when he was drunk. Other times, she gave as good as she got. Many nights, both went to jail charged with "simple battery" under the Domestic Violence Act. The next day, they loved each other again and wanted to drop charges. The judge always reduced the charges to "disorderly conduct" and found them both guilty so they had to pay fines and serve a little jail time. *Same old story.* They were not legally married but had lived together for many years and were considered "common law" married. They had four kids together, ranging in age from three to fifteen. The kids were the biggest victims.

One evening, about six months prior, I had received a call to the medical center. Maggie had taken a hot iron and held it against the side of George's face because he was passed-out drunk. I charged her with "aggravated assault," a felony. George was badly burned and would be scarred for life, but he still loved Maggie and wanted to make things work. He did not want to press charges. *One of these folks is going to eventually kill the other one.*

About three months after the hot-iron incident, I got another call to the hospital. George had slashed Maggie's throat with a box cutter. It made a nasty-looking gash all the way across her throat but wasn't deep enough to be life-threatening. After I took George to jail, charged with "aggravated assault," I went back to the emergency room to talk to Maggie.

"Maggie, why don't you get away from him? Just take the kids and leave. One of you is going to wind up killing the other. When I first met you, I used to charge y'all with disorderly conduct. Then it was simple battery. Now we're up to aggravated assault, Maggie. That's been the progression. You know what it's going to be next time? It's probably gonna be a murder charge. You know it, and I know it."

"I still love him, Officer John. I can't imagine my life without him. Besides, the judge always reduces the charges to disorderly conduct anyway, so…" She shrugged her shoulders.

She was right. I couldn't argue with that. "Just think about your kids and everything y'all are putting them through by staying together," was the only thing I could think to say. "No one has to be there to press charges on a homicide, Maggie. The state presses the charges."

George and Maggie's house was on my beat, about five minutes from the Hardee's. I bagged up the rest of my food and headed out the door. *Well, at least I'm getting called to their house this time and not the emergency room.*

About the same time I thought that, headquarters came back over the radio. "Headquarters to three-twelve, can you respond code two? The caller is advising seventy-one hundred. We're getting you a backup unit. Be advised, seventy-one hundred is by shotgun."

Oh no. One of them has done killed the other one. Seventy-one hundred was the run code for a homicide.

I double-timed it and got to their address in about two and a half minutes. My backup officer, Roz, arrived the same time I did. A small crowd of spectators had already started to form around the front of the house. I ran up to the porch, where I could see the fifteen-year-old daughter sitting Indian-style with Maggie's head in her lap. "Where are your sister and your brothers?" I asked.

The fifteen-year-old looked up at me with tears in her eyes. "I sent them inside the house."

She was cradling Maggie's head in her arms and rocking back and forth. I didn't have the heart to tell her to go inside with the other kids, even though I knew that's what I was supposed to do in order to preserve the crime scene. I looked at Maggie. She was lying face up, her mouth and eyes wide open. Her face had a surprised expression. It also had about eighteen holes from two rounds of buckshot from a twelve-gauge. I didn't need a paramedic or coroner to tell me...she was dead.

"Where's your daddy?"

"He did this. Then he took off. Ran around the corner."

The ambulance was on its way. "Roz," I said. "Stay here with them and secure the scene till the ambulance and detectives get here. I'm going after George."

"You sure? You don't want me to go with you?"

"I'm good. I'll talk to him. He'll listen to me," I replied. I didn't really know if he would, but it sounded good at the time. I took off running in the direction the daughter had pointed. I ran across the shotgun in a neighbor's yard and tried not to step on it. George had dropped it as he was running away. It was a double-barrel sawed-off, so it only held two shots. He had emptied both barrels into Maggie's face.

It didn't take long to catch up to him. George was a large man. He was good bit bigger than I was. He had spent some time lifting weights in prison, but he couldn't run far without getting winded. I hopped a couple of fences and was able to catch up to him two blocks away. He'd slowed to a walk.

"George, stop!" It was the two of us standing out there. There was no one else around.

He turned toward me with this crazy look in his eyes. I don't know how to describe it, but it was scary. I was within twenty feet of him, and he held a knife in his right hand. It looked to be a three-inch folder, a shiny pocket knife. He was breathing hard, like a bull about to charge. I drew my service pistol and pointed it at him. I had my sight picture aimed right at his upper thoracic area. My finger was on the trigger as I spoke. It was just starting to get dark outside.

"George, drop the knife. If you take one step toward me with that knife…" I wanted him to know I would shoot him if I had to. "George, you know me. It's me, John. You know I will listen to your side of the story. George, I don't want to have to hurt you. Drop the knife right now."

I kept saying his name and my name to make us seem like just two guys talking. "George. It's me, John. Talk to me. Tell me what happened. You know we can talk this out. We always have before."

He continued to stare at me. He wasn't dropping it. I started taking the slack out of my trigger. A suspect with a knife can close a distance of twenty feet in one and a half seconds. Even if you shoot him, the suspect might not fall immediately. He can do significant, even fatal, damage after closing the distance. He can swipe that blade all over your body, as if you were caught in a big blender, and you can bleed out.

I probably gave George too many chances and talked to him for too long, but I had faith that he would drop it. Still, I was taking the slack out of my trigger. It felt like it was almost all the way to the rear and the hammer was about to drop when he finally dropped the knife. It's the closest I ever came to killing someone during my career as a cop. I'm glad I didn't have to. I would not have felt good about it, but I was going to go home that night. I was sure about that.

I watched him drop the knife, and he put his open hands out to the sides where I could see them. I released the pressure from my trigger and laid my index finger along the slide. "Good, George. That's progress. Now face away from me and walk toward me backward… slowly."

He turned around to face away from me, the knife still by his feet. He started walking slowly backward toward me. It was exactly what I wanted him to do. I was using my "verbal judo," as they called it at the academy.

My gun was still pointed at him with my right hand, in case he tried anything else, as my left hand started reaching toward my cuffs on the lower left side of my belt. My left hand is my "support" hand. Some people call your off-hand your "weak" hand. I don't call it that because it's not weak if you train it. You should always treat it as your support hand.

"You're doing real good, George. I know we'll be able to talk through this. I want to hear your side of the story. I want you to tell me what happened. George, you're a good bit bigger than me, and I'm here by myself. I'm going to want to handcuff you while we're talking so there's no misunderstanding between us. Is it okay with you?"

I could see him nodding yes. He started bringing his hands down behind his back so I could cuff him. *Wow, this verbal judo is actually working.* I holstered my gun. He was in a position for me to get the cuffs on him; I did it quickly.

Just as I got George cuffed with his hands behind his back, a cop from Bibb City showed up. Bibb City was a small town alongside the Chattahoochee River. It had its own three-officer police force. This cop's name was Tommy, and I did not like working with him. He had shown up on some other calls with me, and while I appreciated his effort to back me up, he had a quick temper. In my opinion, he did not belong on the street with a gun and badge. *Here comes trouble.*

"Tommy, chill out. He's cooperating. We're just talking here," I told him. "Just go and secure the knife on the ground over there."

I had turned George around to face me. I wanted to talk to him and get him to tell me what happened before the transport car showed up to take him to jail. Detectives were already arriving at the crime scene, but I wanted to get George's confession. I read him his Miranda warning. Then I said, "Just talk to me, man. What happened?"

He dropped his big old head and his big shoulders and started to tell me. "Well, Officer John, what had happened was—"

"You shut up! You shut your mouth!" Tommy yelled as he ran up and slapped George across his face.

"Rrraaawwwrrr!" I swear that's the noise George made. He turned into the Incredible Hulk, and I didn't blame him. I would have done the same thing if a man slapped me openhandedly like that.

I yelled at Tommy, "What did you just do?"

Big George, with his hands still cuffed behind his back, head-butted Tommy, breaking his nose. He tried to roundhouse kick me in the face, but I managed to back away in time. This caught him off balance, so I was able to tackle him and pin him facedown to the ground. There was no talking to him now; he was so mad. I would have been too. I still think to this day his kick attempt at me was only a half-hearted gesture. If he really wanted to, he could have connected it, but he liked me because I always treated him fairly.

Tommy was out of commission, but other units had started to arrive. George was uninjured, so we were able to transport him directly to the county jail, but it would be days before he would talk to anyone.

Thanks, Tommy, for your hotheadedness and over-aggressiveness. The only reason I can think of for that was Tommy saw an opportunity to assert some aspect of power over someone bigger than himself. He thought George would be unable to defend himself with his hands cuffed behind his back. He never would have been able to win against someone like George in a one-on-one fair fight. He definitely did not see the head-butt coming.

As a side note, Tommy is no longer a cop. Not because of this incident but because of an accumulation of things. Someone finally realized, "Hey, maybe giving this guy a badge and gun is not a good idea."

It took detectives days of talking to George before he finally confessed to killing Maggie. They didn't really need his confession, as there were plenty of pieces of evidence and witness statements already, but convictions are always easier with a confession.

She'd been nagging him again because he was drunk and needed to get a job. She had told him that she was going to walk next door, get the neighbor's shotgun, and put George out of his misery. In their neighborhood, the doors and windows were open all the time. Neighbors would walk into and out of one another's houses at random.

George was fed up, plus drunk. Alcohol always adds fuel to the fire. He walked next door to borrow the neighbor's double-barrel twelve-gauge. Then he walked up to Maggie, sitting on their front porch in front of all their kids. *Blam! Blam!* That was it. Done. He felt as if he got her before she got him.

My good friend Tim was a cop in East Point, Georgia, just outside of Atlanta, for a number of years. I have to give him credit for telling me this: "John, police work is the same from Savannah to Columbus to East Point to Los Angeles…even all the way to Dublin, Ireland. We all deal with the same absurd, the same funny, the same sad, the same shock. It's all the same characters, just with different names and faces."

Morning Watch

As a young cop at Columbus PD, I discovered a beautiful thing. Most people would call it midnight shift, but we called it morning watch. We went on duty around eleven at night and got off around eight in the morning.

Most people follow their natural circadian rhythms and fall asleep by midnight. That's if they're staying up late. If you're a cop on the morning watch, you might respond to 911 calls for the first two hours of the shift but then it slows way down. Even on payday weekends, the bar fights, the drunken fights, and the domestic calls are mostly over by two in the morning. I used the slow time to go around and check the businesses on my beat.

Before I started working beat twelve, it had a reputation for a high business burglary rate. To me, it wasn't difficult to go around and shake door handles or check windows. Walking the perimeters of some small businesses on my beat was easy, and it helped keep my business burglary rate low. This section of the city had some doctors' offices, pharmacies, and a few mom-and-pop grocery stores in it. After I checked those, I would go around to the gas station convenience stores (the ones that were open twenty-four hours) to check on the clerks. They were always appreciative and would usually buy me a cup of coffee just for stopping in. We had a saying on morning watch: "There are only two kinds of people out at this time of night: the good guys and the bad guys. We're the good guys."

Once, I got called into the patrol lieutenant's office for not issuing enough traffic citations during my morning watch shift. I said, "Lieutenant, look at the amount of arrests I had last month. Crack, heroin, meth...aggravated assault, aggravated battery. Look at the low burglary and robbery stats on my beat. Please don't get onto

me for not writing enough traffic tickets. Is that really what this is about?"

"John, what beat you ride?" (He didn't even know.)

I said, "Beat twelve, sir."

"What major roads on your beat?" (He honestly didn't know. He was an out-of-touch manager, not a leader.)

I had to tell him, "Talbotton Road, Twelfth Avenue, and Veteran's Parkway."

He said, "Oh yeah, they be flying out there, boy. Get us some speeding tickets." He wanted me to sit and run radar, trying to catch speeders.

All this good work I'm doing is being overlooked because I'm not bringing in enough quick money for the city.

Traffic tickets were a quick source of revenue for the city. Our department wouldn't publicly acknowledge having a ticket quota, but they had one. It was unwritten. They wouldn't even tell the officers how many tickets were required each month…just "more." I walked out of his office frustrated, but I followed orders. I started running radar along the major roads on my beat. I caught some speeders, got a few DUI arrests, and caught a couple of people with weed in their car, but it was all pretty lame. The businesses on my beat started getting broken into again, and I had a longer response time to calls because I was out on traffic stops. I felt it was counterproductive, and I always try to avoid counterproductive situations.

My beat was busy because I worked in the ghetto, but after two in the morning, everything seemed to slow down…until Tony came along. Tony was the fugitive squad detective. He was assigned the responsibility of rounding up people who had dodged their court appearances and had outstanding warrants. This was way before Dog the Bounty Hunter had a show on reality TV.

Tony was proactive and realized that the fugitive squad had a huge backlog of people to arrest. He also realized that the officers in my squad were young and aggressive and looking for something to do on the morning watch.

Even fugitives had to sleep sometime. Some were nocturnal animals, like us, but even if they stayed up all night and slept all day,

they were usually hanging out at their last known address in the middle of the night, playing video games, watching movies, or whatever. I looked forward to hearing Tony's voice come over the radio at about two o'clock.

"Four sixty-five to any available section three unit."

Everyone in the section would roger up.

"Meet me at the Marathon convenience store, at Veteran's Parkway and River Road. Four sixty-five is buying coffee."

We all knew what that meant. Jim, Greg, Buddy, and I were all there to meet him within about five minutes. Tony would buy us coffee, and we'd sit and sip while we discussed the houses we were going to hit.

"John, this one's on your beat," he would say. Most of them were either on my beat or Greg's. Many were in the housing projects, but a few were in residential neighborhoods.

After we talked for about twenty minutes about what we were going to do, we'd go out and roll up on the first house. Buddy always went up to the front door with Tony to wake the people up and announce that a warrant was being served. Buddy was the biggest guy in the squad and could bust the front door in, if necessary. I always went around to the backyard with a Remington 870 twelve-gauge, in case the suspects tried to slip out the back door. Jim and Greg kept watch on the sides of the house or apartment building.

Tony passed away in 2007. He died of a sudden massive heart attack, sitting in his easy chair at home, watching television. Heart disease is a leading cause of death within the public safety community. I'll always be grateful for those late-night details where he made good use of our squad. *I wish I could have seen him one last time before he passed away.*

When I worked morning watch, even on my days off, I stayed up all night and slept all day. I was a bona fide day sleeper. Blackout curtains in the bedroom helped. I also tried to find off-duty security work to make some extra money. One midnight part-time job (literally a "moonlighting" job) came by way of an officer named Joel.

A man named Kaparza owned a gravel, sand, and landscaping company on Joel's beat. The property held a lot of large construction

equipment, which kept getting vandalized overnight. Also, the office got broken into repeatedly, even though there was really nothing in there to steal. The perpetrator would just do something creepy, like defecate in the middle of the office floor or on top of a desk.

I don't know if you've had to replace a big tractor tire lately, but if one of those gets slashed, it's big money. So is cleaning the side of a dump truck spray-painted with profanity. If something like this happens a few times a week, it runs into even bigger money. Then there's cleaning human excrement out of the office area. Insurance didn't cover it all.

Kaparza was an older gentleman who had started dating a younger woman. The woman was going through a bad divorce, and Kaparza suspected the soon-to-be ex-husband was the vandal. The officers who worked this beat were able to stop by a few times during a shift, but it was a very large section, and they had many other things to do. They had other calls to take and other businesses to check. They couldn't be there all the time.

Kaparza wanted to hire an off-duty cop to keep watch over his property and equipment. He wanted the officer on site from about ten o'clock at night, right after the last employee left for the evening, until about seven in the morning, when the first employees started showing up to work. Of course, he wanted the officer to keep a low profile. He didn't want his regular employees spooked by the idea of a cop sitting on the property overnight. Joel called me because he knew I'd be interested. He worked the detail himself sometimes but couldn't work it every night. Kaparza was willing to pay thirty dollars an hour. I couldn't resist. I snatched up the opportunity and thanked Joel for offering it.

I could sit in one spot and keep most of the property in sight, kind of like watching for deer from a deer stand. It was cold on this particular night, so I was wearing long johns under my uniform. I had made it onto the SWAT team by then. Following Joel's lead, I decided to wear my tactical uniform: all-black BDU (battle dress uniform).

It was starting to turn daylight: *almost quitting time.* I checked my watch: *almost seven o'clock.* Nothing had happened. I was count-

ing dollar signs in my head. A black pickup truck rolled through the gate, onto the property. My senses perked up, but I knew it might well have been just an employee early for work. Joel had given me a description of Kaparza, but I had never met the man in person.

The pickup truck rolled up to the office and parked, and an older gentleman got out. I guessed it was Kaparza. I wanted to introduce myself and let him know that we were looking out for him. As he started to open the office door, I approached him from the trees and asked, "Excuse me, sir. Are you Mr. Kaparza?" He jumped and dropped his keys.

"Jesus! Yes, I am!"

"Well, sir, I'm not Jesus, but I am one of the officers working on your property here. I just wanted to let you know that you're getting your money's worth. It's been real quiet all night."

"Well, that's good news, officer. Thank you. You can go now. I always want you guys gone by the time my employees start showing up. I don't want any of them asking questions about you."

"I understand, sir," I said. Then I shook his hand and left. This was the sum total of my interaction with Kaparza. Later, he would tell Joel that I snuck up on him in a black uniform, like a ninja, and startled him while he was opening the office. It was the first time I felt as if I'd been thrown under the bus. I've gotten used to it over the years because I basically live under the bus.

Joel called me later while I was back at my house sleeping. "John, you can't be sneaking up on our customer like that. He was all freaked out."

"Joel, look, I didn't sneak up on him for one thing. I announced myself from a pretty good distance away, like we're supposed to. Does he not realize we're there until seven o'clock, and he might run into one of us if he shows up early? He shouldn't be so jumpy."

The next couple of times I worked the detail, I tried to figure out how I could see the morning's first employees showing up for work and slip out without being seen. I parked my patrol car about a quarter mile away at an abandoned carwash. We had a "take-home car" program at CPD. We could drive our city-issued cars home

when we were off-duty. We were allowed to drive them to and from work, training, and part-time jobs.

I'd drive my patrol car to the abandoned carwash, park it, and walk the quarter mile to the job site. I did my best to sneak onto the property through the woods by around ten o'clock, when the last employee was locking up for the night. The workers never knew I was there. I always waited until I saw the first one show up the next morning, usually around seven o'clock. Then I'd sneak off the property and walk back to my car.

The last time I worked the detail, I was back at my house when Joel called. "Hey, what happened last night?"

"Nothing," I said. "It was quiet all night. I was there until the first employee showed up this morning."

"Well, some of the tractor tires got slashed."

"Are you joking?" was all I could think to say. I thought he was messing with me at first, but he was serious.

I had watched the property like a hawk all night. My theory is that the perp knew we were working security there. I don't know how, but he knew. He was watching us, watching for him. Maybe he even knew where I parked my patrol car. He didn't want a confrontation, obviously. He must have done the damage while the first employee was getting settled into the office after I'd left. However it went down, it was on me. The damage had been done on my watch.

I told Joel that I didn't want to work the detail anymore. If I had seen someone slashing tractor tires on the property, obviously, I would have confronted him. But I didn't see him. He timed his activities perfectly. They never did catch the vandal.

Scoffers set a city aflame, but the wise turn away wrath.

World Trade Center Attacks

Shortly after the whole Kaparza fiasco, I had returned home from my regular morning watch shift and changed out of my uniform into my sleep shorts. Kim and I were married by then and had a four-year-old son.

Kim and I had dated on and off throughout high school and college. We met through mutual friends in eleventh grade, started talking and hanging out, and then started dating. We would break up, make up, and get back together. Usually, it was my fault we had broken up. We went to our senior prom together and graduated from high school in 1990. I knew I was in love with her when she kissed me at the prom.

One of the times we got back together, we were twenty-two and figured maybe we were meant to be together. Kim worked as a daytime office manager at an Applebee's and took nursing classes at night, so I figured she was a good girl and a keeper. Besides, I was crazy about her. She attended my graduation from the police academy in 1993, so I felt it was a good sign that things were serious between us.

I asked her to marry me. Even though she was out of my league, she said yes. We were married in 1994. I always tell people I tricked her into marrying me. She's smarter, funnier, and better looking than I am. I feel blessed to have her because she could have had any man she wanted, but she picked me.

Two years after we were married, Kim started having dizzy spells. I kept telling her it wasn't normal, and she needed to go see a doctor, but she wouldn't listen to me. The spells went on for about six months, varying in frequency and severity. One evening, she stood up from the dinner table and fell straight over. I was able to

catch her before she hit the floor. I said, "That's it. We're going to the emergency room." I carried her to the car and drove her to St. Francis Hospital. *God, please don't take my wife away. If you have to take one of us, take me instead.*

After a series of tests, the doctors realized she was going into V-tach (ventricular tachycardia) whenever the dizzy spells occurred. Her heartbeat was irregular, and they were able to determine it was being caused by some scar tissue that had built up around the wall of one of the chambers in her heart. She'd been diagnosed with a case of strep throat the year prior. More than likely what happened was some of the strep virus traveled through her bloodstream into her heart and caused the damage.

The doctors performed a relatively new procedure on Kim. They put two catheters through the arteries in her left thigh: one had a camera on the tip; the other had a cauterizing iron. Once inserted through her thigh and into her heart chamber, they were able to smooth the scar tissue down by cauterizing it. She recovered over the course of the next week. They ran her through several stress tests and gave her a clean bill of health. No matter what they did to her, they could not induce the V-tach or dizzy spells. It was a miracle procedure. It worked exactly as the doctors had expected. Leading up to this, Kim and I had been talking about trying to have a baby soon, but I was afraid the stress of childbirth would be too much strain on her heart. I didn't want to come close to losing her again. The doctors assured me that they would keep an eye on it, but it should not be a concern. A year later in 1997, we had our son.

Nick was four years old when 9/11 happened. I always slept with the television on because the background noise helped me sleep. Around a quarter to nine o'clock, I had started to doze off when the first plane hit the north tower of the World Trade Center. The announcer came on with breaking news, a sense of urgency in his voice, and a video clip of the plane crashing into the building. I was confused. *Was this an accident?* I couldn't go back to sleep now. Then the second plane hit the south tower. *That's no accident.* Our nation was under attack. Kim was at work, and Nick was at daycare. I called Kim to find out if she was watching. She was; the whole country was watching.

For about two months prior, I had been feeling an urge or a calling to do something more than just serve the city of Columbus, Georgia. I had submitted an application with a company called DynCorp. They recruited American cops to serve on an International Police Task Force. The IPTF was a program that allowed any sworn police officer or deputy sheriff in the United States to apply to serve in Bosnia or Kosovo and help train their new police forces. Those two countries were emerging from civil wars. The new police officers there needed training on how laws are enforced in democratic societies. It seemed like exactly what I was looking for.

I had attended an FBI job fair about a year prior and had submitted an application, but they weren't interested in me. I was a twenty-eight-year-old white male with a bachelor's degree in criminal justice and didn't speak any foreign languages. I was a dime a dozen in their eyes and met only the minimum qualifications to apply. They didn't care that I had worked for Columbus PD for ten years. If I was serious about wanting to be an FBI agent, I should have learned a foreign language fluently or received an advanced degree. That's how they saw it.

The American contingent of the International Police Task Force was a US State Department detail, operating as part of a larger United Nations peacekeeping mission. DynCorp had been contracted by the State Department to recruit, conduct background checks on, hire, and pay qualified American officers. They were offering $90,000 over the course of a one-year contract. It seemed like an incredible opportunity to answer a higher calling and pay off some debt at the same time. The only catch was that I would have to resign from CPD. The department wouldn't allow me to take a one-year leave of absence. It had a "no rehire" policy in place. If I resigned, there was no going back.

During the days and weeks following 9/11, people were extremely apprehensive about air travel. DynCorp had a large contingent of American police officers preparing to end their missions in Bosnia and Kosovo as well as East Timor. It was the end of the fiscal year, and those officers' contracts were ending. Many would-be replacement officers backed out or canceled their contracts at the

last minute because of 9/11. I had done some independent research about each of those countries; all of them had terrorist training camps sprinkled throughout. *As long as I'm doing the right thing, God will look out for me.*

Having Faith

My faith in God hasn't always been as strong as it is now. I've gone through many periods of my life, or seasons, during which I found myself questioning His very existence. When I was a cop especially, I saw some of the worst things people can do to one another up close and personal. No one ever calls the police because something good happened. It's just different degrees of bad. Dealing with the bad day in and day out for a number of years causes a person to develop a dark sense of humor.

I wouldn't say I was ever an atheist. I didn't deny or disbelieve God's existence. I would say I was more an agnostic at one point. I was a doubter. I didn't claim disbelief, but I didn't claim faith either. *If there is a God, then why does He let such horrible things happen to good people?* Much of my twenties were spent asking that question.

Jesus is a historical figure. He did walk the earth and preach the gospel, but was He really the Son of God or just another prophet? I wasn't sure. Were the stories in the Bible factual? I had read it from cover to cover, but I didn't know. Did He truly rise from the dead, ascend into Heaven, and is He really coming back? I doubted all of it.

Because you are lukewarm, neither hot nor cold, I am about to spit you out.

Having children brings a glimmer of hope; it did for me anyway. The whole pregnancy and childbirth experience is a miracle in itself. Then you see something in your children, and it makes you feel positive about the future of mankind on a grander scale. They're little people you shape and in whom you instill your values.

Around the year 2000, when Nick was three, I knew I needed to set a good example and be a role model for my son. Kim and I tossed around the idea of having another baby. But we didn't want

two kids in college at the same time (thinking toward the future), so we decided to wait until Nick was five or six. We also found a church we loved and started attending every Sunday. I started tithing, which I had never done before.

A generous person will prosper; whoever refreshes others will be refreshed.

I started reading my Bible again and set time aside to pray every day. I asked God and Jesus to come back into my life and take control. I told God I loved Him and expressed how much I wanted to be close to Him again. I thanked Him for sending His Son, Jesus, to pay the debt for our sins. I began to realize we are all God's children, but He doesn't want us to love Him from afar. He wants His children to climb right up onto His lap, hug and kiss Him, and ask for big important things, just as any good father would. A sense of peace came over me, and answers to my questions started coming to me. I began to feel a sense of guidance.

For God so loved the world that He gave His one and only son, that whoever believes in Him shall not perish, but have eternal life.

I also started reading works by C. S. Lewis. I read an interview with him once, during which the interviewer asked, "Why do you think the righteous suffer?"

Lewis replied, "Why shouldn't they suffer? They're the only ones who can handle it."

DynCorp called me one week after 9/11. I was about to become a United States government (USG) contractor.

Suit up in the full armor of God: sword of the spirit, shield of faith, breastplate of righteousness, helmet of salvation, belt of truth, and boots of peace.

First Flight to Dulles

I had to take care of a few administrative tasks at CPD before I could sign a contract with DynCorp. I let them know that I intended to resign, first of all, and asked them to send a copy of my personnel record over to DynCorp. I also needed qualifying shooting scores that were less than three months old. I hadn't requalified in about five months.

I called my SWAT sergeant, and he agreed to meet me at the firearms range. He had the day off, but he told me he understood my desire to go out and do something bigger and better. He said he wished he'd done the same thing when he was younger. It made me feel good and gave me a sense of pride. It provided encouragement when I was at a figurative crossroads. *Thanks, Sarge.*

He stopped by the armory to pick up my MP-5 and AR-15, along with ammo for those weapons. He also brought spare .45 ammo for my sidearm. All I had to do was show up at the range with my service pistol and eye and ear protection. We were only there for about an hour, just long enough for me to shoot qualifying scores with each weapon. Now I had an official piece of paper signed by my SWAT sergeant that I could send to DynCorp. Next thing I knew I was on an airplane from Atlanta to Washington Dulles.

It was September 28, 2001, seventeen days after 9/11. It was my Uncle Mike's thirty-sixth birthday. Uncle Mike is a Detroit firefighter who went to New York to help clean up Ground Zero. He's only seven years older than I am, but I always looked up to him, and he's always been more like a big brother to me. He actually saved my life once, which I'll tell more about in a later chapter.

Kim and Nick dropped me off at Atlanta's Hartsfield-Jackson International Airport. Security was extremely tight for days, weeks,

and months after 9/11. The Bush administration was still trying to figure out how it had happened and how we could prevent it from happening again.

My bags were searched thoroughly. My wife and I distinctly remember the security person unpacking all of my clothes, right down to the last pairs of underwear and socks, and unfolding them out onto the table. When the security officer finished checking them, he just stuffed my clothes back into my bags. It was like going through an airport in some third-world country. He turned my bags upside down and shook them out. I walked through the metal detector, got patted down, wanded, and patted down again. *I'm an American cop, for Pete's sake.* Everyone was treated like a potential threat. We think we have it bad going through airport security now. Try to remember what the nation's sentiment was like right after 9/11.

I understood why the airport security personnel were so thorough. Even though I didn't like it, I remained calm and went through the required procedures. I had been through worse things in my young life. I was almost twenty-nine and had already seen some of the worst things humans can do to one another. I knew there was something better waiting for me on the other side of this plane ride.

DynCorp had informed me that if I passed their two-week intense training-and-vetting course, I would deploy to Kosovo immediately. There would be no going home after that. I would sign a one-year contract, and I honestly didn't know when Kim and Nick dropped me off at the airport whether I would see them again for a whole year. Nick was only four. That was tough. Plus, we had an old dog named Zak. He was the best dog I've ever had, but he'd already been with us for a long time, and I didn't know if I'd ever see him again.

I started to get emotional as I said goodbye to Kim and Nick. I hugged and kissed them at the check-in area. Most young people don't even know this, but your loved ones used to be able to walk you all the way to your departure gate. I remember once, when I was a little kid, they even let me onto the plane to hug my dad one last time when he was flying away somewhere. (I don't even remember where now. It was probably Dugway, Utah. My dad had to train in

Dugway often during the 1980s because the terrain was similar to Afghanistan. Those old enough to remember the Russians occupying Afghanistan, or who have seen the movie or read the book *Charlie Wilson's War*, will know what I'm talking about.)

Accompanying loved ones to their departure gates ended after 9/11. Only ticket-holding passengers were allowed past the check-in area after that. As I said goodbye to my wife and son, I knew I was doing the right thing. I made sure they understood it too.

This is the right move to make, I'm sure of it. I can't back down now. Be strong and courageous, for the Lord will be with you wherever you go.

First Contract

I stepped off the plane at Washington Dulles International Airport and followed the instructions DynCorp had given me. This was the first time I had ever flown into Dulles. I didn't realize it at the time, but this would be the first of many flights in and out of that airport for me. I picked up my bags at the designated carousel. I'd packed surprisingly light considering I expected to go away for a whole year.

I noticed a guy who'd gotten off the same plane I had. He picked up his luggage at the same carousel and was walking toward the same designated meeting point. I decided to make a friend.

"Hey, maybe you're going to meet the same people I am. I'm John, from Columbus PD." I stuck my hand out to shake his hand. Cops have a way of recognizing one another even in plain clothes.

"I'm Scott, APD," he said back. Every cop in Georgia knows APD meant he worked in Atlanta. Scott gave me a good firm handshake with his great big paw and said, "Are you heading to meet the DynCorp people?"

"Yeah," I replied. "I figured you probably were too."

Scott said, "Well, let's go see what this is all about, brother."

Scott and I were among the first to show up near the designated meeting point, so we had to stand around and wait a while. We waited for about two hours while other officers' flights arrived. About eighty people were expected to show up for this vetting course. A few had missed their flights, and some flights were delayed, but those of us who arrived on time were eventually walked outside and loaded onto buses. They drove us to a Residence Inn in Fredericksburg, Virginia, where we would spend the next two weeks. No one really talked much during the hour-long bus ride.

Once we arrived, each of us was assigned a roommate. Males were paired with males; females with females. One married couple, both cops, would be rooming together. A father-and-son team was paired up. I hoped to be rooming with Scott because we were both from Georgia and about the same age. I wanted to pick his brain about what it was like to work in Atlanta, but the room assignments were in alphabetical order by last name. My last name is Cassel, and his started with an *R*, so it wasn't likely that we'd be rooming together. I was paired with Rocky Brown, an older cop from Tennessee. He seemed okay. He had done a mission to Kosovo before, so I took advantage of the opportunity to learn a little about what to expect once we got over there.

Rocky told me that living in Kosovo was kind of like "urban camping." I asked him what he meant by that. As I understood it, you lived in whichever major city you were assigned to: Pristina, Mitrovica, Peja, Prizren, or Gjilani. He had been assigned to Gjilani and was going to try to get back there again. *What aspect of living in an urban area could be considered camping?*

He explained that the electricity and water systems went out often. Whichever house or apartment you chose to rent was referred to as an "accommodation." It was best to have a generator at your accommodation and some type of propane or kerosene heater during the winter months. Also, when the water was turned off for days at a time, you might have to take a bath with bottled water. I had never dealt with any of that before.

When the water was on, it was okay to shower, wash clothes, and wash dishes with, but you definitely didn't want to drink it. In fact, while showering, it was best to avoid letting it get into your eyes and mouth. You would also probably want to brush your teeth with bottled water. Apparently, the tap water in Kosovo did (and still does) contain a high concentration of human DNA from all the dead bodies floating in the lakes and rivers during the war. *Okay, now this guy is just trying to freak me out. I'm sorry I asked.*

During his previous mission there, Rocky had been assigned as a field training officer (FTO), working with a couple of Albanian cops fresh out of the academy. I had worked as an FTO toward the

end of my tenure at CPD. I wondered if there was a language barrier. He explained that most of the younger Albanians spoke at least enough English to carry on a decent conversation. Many of the older ones did not because they hadn't been taught English in school. I also wanted to know how dangerous it was to work there. Rocky said, of course, it's best to be on guard all the time and maintain your situational awareness, but it was not any more dangerous than working as a cop in the States. The war was over.

I unpacked and settled into the room. I tried to get to bed early and get a decent night's sleep. We had to be dressed in PT (physical training) gear and standing in formation by the buses by seven o'clock the next morning. I felt so anxious; I found it difficult to fall asleep. It didn't help that Rocky snored like a chainsaw. Before he fell asleep, he told me that many officers would probably be cut from this initial training course. They would be sent home. He'd seen it before.

"A lot of these guys and gals you see here now, they won't be here by the end of next week."

How difficult can it be? Rocky was twenty years older than I was, and he had a bit of a potbelly. If he could pass the course, I knew I could. Failure was not an option for me; I didn't have a job to go back to in Georgia.

I wanted to do well at this training and vetting course and wanted to get these next two weeks over with so I could deploy to Kosovo. They called it a "training and vetting course" because while they were going to teach us things we needed to know, they were also going to be evaluating and weeding people out as necessary.

I said a little prayer before I finally drifted off to sleep.

Go, therefore, and make disciples of all nations, baptizing them in the name of the Father, the Son, and the Holy Spirit.

The Crucible

ynCorp had subcontracted a global solutions company to train us on how to operate in third-world countries. Every day for the next two weeks was strictly regimented. The PT was rigorous, more so than it had been at my police academy. I didn't want to feel full or get sick during it, so I didn't eat anything at breakfast, only drank coffee and water. We would line up in formation at seven o'clock. Some of the officers got injured or couldn't keep up, so they were sent home.

We would then load up onto the buses in our sweaty PT clothes and ride over to the training facility in the sticks near Fredericksburg. It was called the Crucible and was about a twenty-minute bus ride from our hotel. Once we arrived, we were given an opportunity to shower quickly and change into blue BDUs. When I was issued a set of dog tags with my name, social security number, blood type, and religious preference, the reality set in. I, or some of my compatriots here, might not come home in one piece. Some of the officers chose not to wear the dog tags. I wore mine faithfully.

A good part of each day was spent shooting on the range and then beating the crap out of one another at hand-to-hand combat. A couple of days were spent practicing "enhanced baton tactics." I had been through similar training, but this was much more intense. The instructors at the Crucible were training us to protect ourselves in a third-world country where stakes were higher and the rules of engagement were much less strict.

Some of the officers couldn't make the shooting standards and were cut from the course. Others were injured during the practical scenarios. There was usually a quick lunch break around noon where a catering crew would bring in sandwiches and bottled water. The

abuse would resume after lunch. I was "embracing the suck." My good friend Kris always says, "Whenever you have to go through something that sucks…just embrace the suck, bro." He'd been through Army Ranger School.

The Lord is greater than the giants you face. This is nothing; it's only two weeks. Failure is not an option here. Quitting is not an option here. Are you a sheep or a sheepdog? I am a sheepdog protecting my flock.

Our days would usually end around six o'clock, and we would be transported back to the hotel to eat dinner, regroup, and prepare for the next day. The DynCorp administrators would be waiting for us back at the hotel. They would visit certain officers' rooms during the evening to let them know they had underperformed during some of the practical exercises. Those officers were cut from the course and sent home.

I sat with the same group of guys each morning in the dining hall, sipping my coffee. We noticed that the herd was thinning. Every morning, there were fewer and fewer officers boarding the buses. I took a look around. Rocky was still there. Scott was still there. Scott's roommate, a big corn-fed Texas cop named Brandon (we all called him Tex) was still there. *We must have lost at least twenty people so far.*

Toward the end of the two weeks, a psychologist came in to interview each of us individually. I don't know what he was looking for, other than obvious mental instability or sociopathic tendencies, but he weeded out a few more people. DynCorp did not want to take a chance on anyone the shrink considered a risk. There had recently been a scandal in the news involving some officers they'd deployed to Bosnia. Those guys were dirty and started participating in a human-trafficking ring once they got in country. The company didn't have anything to do with the criminal activity itself, but their name was still in the news attached to that scandal.

On the very last day of training at the Crucible, right at the end of the day, we were congratulated by our Crucible instructors and by the DynCorp administrators. We had passed. Now it was time to sign on the dotted line committing ourselves to one year in Kosovo as international police officers for the State Department. They explained that they would pay for two flights: one flight to get

us to Kosovo and one return flight to the States at the end of the year. If we opted to stay and keep working, we could sign on for an additional year. *I could possibly be there for two years total: 2001 to 2003.*

While in-country, we would earn what they called compensatory time off (CTO). It was basically rest and relaxation time. We could spend those off-days in Kosovo or pay for our own flights to wherever we chose. For every three months worked, we earned three weeks of CTO. There were no weekends or holidays off. In fact, there would be no days off at all while in country. We would work every day, eight- to twelve-hour shifts, and on-call as needed. They would deposit five thousand dollars a month into our bank accounts at home. It would be plenty to take care of Kim and Nick. It was more than double my CPD salary.

They would also pay us two thousand five hundred euros a month, cash in hand. It was our mission subsistence allowance. Rent and food in Kosovo was cheap, so I would have plenty left at the end of each month. I felt as if I'd won the lottery.

We filed into the classroom and sat down at our desks. There was a contract and a pretty DynCorp pen on each desk. I didn't even read the fine print; I was so ready to get on the plane. I sat down and signed mine immediately.

Scott's roommate, Tex, stood up from his desk before anyone else. He carried his contract up to the administrator standing at the front of the classroom. A brief conversation took place, though I couldn't make out what they were saying. Tex handed his blank contract over to the administrator and exited the room. He hadn't signed it. He was gone just like that. He had been through these past two weeks with us, right until the end, and then just headed home. The homesickness had gotten to him. He had not even been outside of his small town in Texas in many years and was already missing his family and friends. I looked over at Scott. We just shrugged at each other. The words of a Ronism passed through my head: *It's all over now but the cryin'.*

One of the administrators was waiting outside and drove Tex back to the hotel so that he could quickly and quietly gather his belongings. Then they drove him to Dulles and bought him a plane

ticket headed back to Texas. We never saw him again. We all liked him and felt bad he would not be deploying with us. I guess he was doing what he felt was right for himself and his family. I hope he's doing well and feels as if he made the right choice.

Out of the eighty officers we started with at the Crucible, fifty-five ended up on the plane to Kosovo. Close to one-third of the class had gone home.

I will fear no evil; for you are with me. Your rod and your staff, they comfort me.

First Month in Country

O nce we got to Kosovo, we checked into the UN Hotel. It was comfortable enough and we had our own rooms, but they were tiny and basic. Each had a bed, a closet, a toilet, and a sink. You had to walk down the hall in order to take a shower in the shower stalls. The setup reminded me of a jail cell. There was a coin-operated Laundromat in the basement. We were allowed to stay for three weeks at a rate of two hundred euros a week while we attended the in-service academy.

At the UNMIK (United Nations Mission in Kosovo) academy, we took care of a lot of administrative tasks. For an American cop, and most cops who policed in first-world countries, it was a refresher on standards, ethics, legal, and sensitivity training. It's all necessary training but also quite boring. Most cops from the NATO member states do not need to be reminded of the standard guidelines for use of force against resisting subjects, but many of the people we would be working with would be police officers from third-world countries. Some were brutal. They would think nothing of beating down a civilian in the middle of the street just for talking back. There would be no multimillion-dollar lawsuits, no settlements, and no apologies.

I was fortunate the Kosovo peacekeeping mission was an English-speaking one. The internationals had to be able to speak English in order to work there. I would not be required to learn a foreign language. The internationals always called us "lazy Americans" for not at least trying. I took the Border Patrol's artificial language test one time and scored 99 percent. I know I have the ability to speak a second language fluently; I've just never taken the time to learn.

My dad was stationed in Germany with the First Infantry Division when I was ten. My family and I lived there for three years.

Plus, I'd taken two years of German in high school so I can speak a little German. (Actually, I understand it better than I can speak it.) By no means am I fluent. This made for a few comical moments when I worked with a couple of the German Polizei who either didn't realize, or had forgotten, that I could understand much of what they were saying. They would banter back and forth with one another in German, mostly talking trash about our teammates, and I would respond to their banter in English. They looked at me with astonished and slightly embarrassed expressions. Then we'd have a good laugh about it.

Speaking a little German came in handy a few times while interacting with the Kosovo Albanian civilians. Many of the older ones did not speak English, and I definitely cannot speak Albanian. However, most of them could speak and understand some German.

At the beginning of the in-service academy, none of us knew whether we'd be staying in the capital city of Pristina or transferring to one of the other cities, which made apartment-hunting seem pointless. We knew that most of the cops in our class would be staying in Pristina to mentor Albanian partner officers through the field qualification portion of their training. A small percentage of us would be transferred to the outlying provinces. An even smaller number would be recruited by the Special Operations Group (SOG).

Because I had some tactical SWAT experience from Columbus PD, I was recruited by the SOG, which meant I would be staying in Pristina. I was thankful they let me know early because it gave me time to go out and find a small efficiency accommodation. My landlord and landlady were an old Albanian couple who didn't speak any English, but they did speak some German. I was able to get by well enough to work out basic landlord/tenant issues. I paid them five hundred euros a month for the whole two years I lived there.

This is all working out brilliantly. For the Lord is my shepherd. I lack nothing.

The Close Protection Unit

I had to attend another tough training course, five-weeks long, for the Close Protection Unit (CPU). There were a dozen of us altogether, including my new friend, Scott. Upon successful completion of the course, our job would be to provide Secret Service–style protection to the lawyers, judges, and politicians who would be overseeing the war crimes trials in Kosovo. We would be close protection officers, also known as a protective security detail. This job would not be easy, so the five-week course was another "gut check" to make sure we had the fortitude and really wanted to be there.

We sucked up the early mornings and late nights. We sucked up the long runs in full gear and the punitive push-ups. I was embracing the suck factor, once again. Assignment to the CPU taught me new skills—some things I had never been trained on when I was on SWAT in Columbus. We learned walking and vehicle protection drills and learned how to respond in case of an attack on our "protectee." We practiced evacuation drills and small-unit shoot, move, and communication tactics. We ran through various attack scenarios, over and over, until I was dreaming about them in my sleep. We shot the qualification course daily with our issued Berettas.

I had never worked with a sidearm that had a "de-cocking" lever, so it took some getting used to. My previous sidearm had always been double-action-only (DAO), but this Beretta was double-action/single-action (DA/SA). With a DAO pistol, you don't have to do anything except take your finger off the trigger before you re-holster. With a DA/SA, the hammer and trigger remain cocked to the rear after your first shot. You have to remember to press the de-cocking lever prior to re-holstering. I developed a technique of re-holstering

with my thumb covering the back of the slide so that I could feel whether the hammer was up or down.

When you re-holster your sidearm, you should never have to look down at your holster or feel for it with your support hand. This is important to me, so I'll share it with you. You should know where your holster is and be able to put your gun back without looking or feeling for it. It should not have moved since your weapon was drawn from it. Your eyes should be up, maintaining situational awareness, and looking around for more threats. You might have to bring your weapon back up and engage more targets.

They taught us a pistol draw technique I had never used, though once I learned it, it made perfect sense. It's been my pistol draw ever since. Your strong hand goes fast to your pistol while your support hand comes to your chest, ready to receive the pistol for a solid two-handed grip. Then, your strong hand slows down and gets a proper grip on your pistol. Finally, you draw your pistol fast from the holster. They called it the fast-slow-fast-draw. As soon as the muzzle of your sidearm clears the top of the holster, you pivot the pistol so that the barrel points toward the target. This way you can shoot from the hip, if necessary. With some practice, you'd be surprised at how many shots you can get on a close, advancing adversary. If the target is far enough away, you punch your pistol straight out toward it and get your sight picture, as well as a solid two-handed grip.

We also shot the qualification course daily with my old friend, the MP-5. It had been my weapon of choice during my days on the SWAT team. They also trained us to use a particular model of long rifle, which I had not handled before, a G-36. I was familiar with the American Colt version of an AR-15, but this was different. It was a very good, reliable weapon system that I would need to learn and get used to carrying. We practiced clearing weapon malfunctions with each system and became proficient at tactical reloads, as well as speed reloads. We drilled them over and over until our hands and fingers blistered and bled. Then we drilled some more.

I knew that my main weakness would be the driving portion of the course, not because I was a bad driver but because I had hardly ever driven a manual transmission vehicle. All the Toyota 4Runners

and most of the Landcruisers assigned to the unit were stick shifts. My city-issued cars back home and all of my personally owned vehicles had been automatic. It was something I hadn't prepared for.

In my spare time, I would borrow a 4Runner from the SOG motor pool and practice my driving and shifting techniques. It had been a long time since I'd driven a stick shift, and I wasn't very good at it. I was able to pass the escape-and-evade portion of the course, just barely. I figured out that I needed to get my RPMs up high, shift fast, and then quickly get my shifting hand back on the steering wheel for positive control of the vehicle.

My goal was to become one of the best drivers in the unit. I became aggressive in my driving style, but I never got into a wreck, and no one ever got hurt. There was a time I almost slid off the side of a curvy mountain road, which was covered with snow and ice. I was able to recover at the last minute and feel as if God was watching out for me on that one. I'm from Georgia, so I wasn't used to driving on snow and ice.

"Man, Cassie. That was a close one." I heard that from my teammates often. I took it as a compliment.

"But did you die?" was always my reply.

My teammates and many of our protectees specifically requested me to drive during protective details. I learned that if you can drive quickly and aggressively, but not wreck out, and get your detail where it needs to be on schedule, you're a rock star. Many other drivers could not do it without wrecking a vehicle. Some chose to drive slowly and carefully, like my grandpa. Not good on a protective detail. There had to be a happy balance.

It was, in fact, difficult for me to ramp my driving style back down once I got back to the states. My wife gave me a few reprimands for driving in Georgia the same way I drove in Kosovo.

First Raid in Country

I t was early February, 2002. I had not seen my family in four
months, the longest I'd ever been away from them. I wasn't able
to make it home for Thanksgiving, Christmas, or New Year's. It
was the first time I'd missed all the holidays. Zak, our old dog, passed
away during that first four months I was gone. I took it really hard
when Kim told me.

It was freezing cold outside; Kosovo had some of the coldest
winters I'd ever experienced. The power was out at my accommoda-
tion a majority of the time, so I had to rely on a kerosene heater and
a small wood-burning stove. I was ready to go home for a few weeks.
I would be home by Valentine's Day. A lot of guys would go home
for their first CTO and not come back. They would e-mail DynCorp
to inform them that they were breaking contract and not returning.
Living conditions in Kosovo took some adjustment. Now I knew
what Rocky meant when he called it urban camping.

The week before my first CTO, I was tasked with participating
in my first warrant service in Kosovo. I had been on drug raids when
I was on SWAT back home, but it had been a while. I felt rusty and
didn't know if I was ready for it. This felt different somehow.

In addition to our daily duties of escorting lawyers and judges
to and from the war crime trials, the Close Protection Unit would
also augment other tactical teams in the Special Operations Group.
The Albanian Organized Crime Unit would call on Team Six some-
times to help them serve high-risk warrants.

Team Six was a special operations squad made up of officers from
several different countries. They had all served for at least three years on
full-time SWAT teams back home. I wanted to be a Team Six member,
but Columbus PD's SWAT officers were only a part-time force, and

I'd only been on SWAT for two years. I didn't qualify to apply. Most of their members were from a German counter-terrorism task force and a Czechoslovakian anti-corruption tactical team. Team Six was small, so CPU sometimes augmented their team during big raids.

A high-ranking Kosovo Albanian police official was suspected of corruption and involvement in organized crime. Scott and I were looking forward to helping out with this because it would be a nice break from our daily protective details. We rolled up on this Albanian guy's house at two in the morning. *My favorite time to roll up on a bad guy's house.* All the lights were out, and it looked as if everyone was sleeping. We announced ourselves briefly and then smashed in the front door with a battering ram. I was the first one through the door, carrying my MP-5. The guy's wife and kids were sleeping on the floor in the front room. The wife immediately woke up and jumped up to protect her kids; I didn't blame her. She started yelling at me in Albanian, and I tried to calm her as best I could in English. The kids were crying, wondering what was going on. They were surrounded by police officers clad in black tactical gear and wearing balaclavas over their heads and faces.

Scott was right behind me carrying the trusty G-36. The husband, the guy we were looking for, came shuffling around the corner of the front room. I looked at his hands. They were empty. He was wearing a t-shirt and boxer shorts and looked as if he'd just jumped out of bed. He was unarmed, but he still came at me as if he was going to try to disarm me. He's lucky he didn't get shot. I struck him in his mouth with the barrel of my machine pistol just to let him know we were there to conduct business. His knees buckled, and his lip bled, soaking down into the front of his white T-shirt. I ordered him to get down on his knees and to put his hands behind his back. He didn't fight. He knew the game was over. Scott kept watch over the room while I cuffed the suspect with plastic flex cuffs. More officers came in behind us to clear the rest of the house.

Once the suspect was secure, I helped clear the rest of the house while Scott stayed with the wife and kids. There was one bedroom we wanted to search, but the door was locked. It was an odd-looking door. It didn't fit in with the rest of the house and was obviously an

afterthought. It reminded me of those grey metal doors you'd see on a utility room or janitor's closet. It was solid but had a two foot by one foot vented opening toward the bottom. Thin metal louvers covered the opening.

We tried smashing the whole thing in with a battering ram, but it would not give. It was more solid than the front door had been. I suggested the breacher smash out just the vented opening, so he did. I put my gloves on to protect my hands from the jagged pieces of metal. I generally did not operate with gloves on back then because I liked to handle my weapon systems with bare hands and fingers, but I always kept a pair of gloves in a pocket close by. It was just my personal preference. There have been a lot of advances in glove technology since then. I've since figured out that I can operate in a pair of snug-fitting neoprene gloves with the thumb and index finger cut out of each.

I announced to the rest of the team that I would fit through the opening at the bottom of the door. No one argued. My MP-5 went through the opening first, and I took a quick peek. The Crucible instructors had told us not to take quick peeks. *If your eyes go that way, and your gun goes that way, then you go that way. Don't give up ground that you've gained.* I thought, in this case, they would be okay with me making an exception.

It was dark in there, so I lit the room with my weapon-mounted flashlight. I started to crawl through and kept looking around to see if there was anything in the room that could kill me. The gear around my waist would not fit through the opening, so I reached up and unlocked the door, then climbed back out. I announced to the rest of the team that the door was open now, so they went in and cleared the room. There were no threats in there, but they did find most of the incriminating evidence and a significant cache of illegal weapons. It was obvious that the corrupt Albanian policeman had kicked his kids out of their bedroom and made them sleep on the cold living room floor so he'd have a room in which to lock away his criminal activity.

I felt as if a higher power was protecting me that night. I sat on the floor in the hallway while the rest of the team cleared the room. I was almost in tears as I said a quiet prayer. I was tired, mentally and

emotionally, and I still had a long way to go. I gave thanks to God that nothing had hurt me.

Do not worry about anything; instead, pray about everything. Tell Him what you need, and thank Him for all He has done.

Grenade Explosion

Scott and I were working a protective detail along with a Norwegian, a Finnish guy, and a Brit. Scott was the team leader, and I was the shift lead on this detail. The Finn was the lead car driver, the Brit was the follow car driver, and the Norwegian was rear gunner. Team Charlie and Team Echo were combined for this detail because the unit was shorthanded once again. Too many officers were away on CTO at the same time.

Our task was to travel to Mitrovica, pick up a Serbian politician from his house, and transport him to his campaign headquarters so that he could give a speech to his supporters. There was a big election coming up, and this guy was a frontrunner in the polls. It was November 2002.

Scott and the Norwegian planned to stay inside the venue with our Serbian protectee. I walked in with them to help make sure the venue was secure, but I wanted to pop back outside. Something seemed out of sorts. My "Spidey senses" were tingling. I wanted to remind our drivers to be extra vigilant. I wanted to tell them in person, not over the radio. Radio silence was only to be broken in an emergency. Sometimes officers got complacent once we arrived at a venue. They might start texting on their phones and what not. Something about this detail just did not feel quite right to me; it felt "cold" somehow. I believe experience plus expertise equals intuition. Intuition is knowing without knowing how you know.

As I walked toward the front entrance of the building, I heard a distinct *boom* from outside in the parking lot. I prayed it was not one of our vehicles. The Brit came over the radio, "Cassie, Southside, we need to go!" There was a sense of urgency in his voice I'd never heard before.

The training kicked in. I rogered up on the radio and ran back to link up with Scott and the Norwegian near the podium where the principal was standing. He had already started to give his campaign speech.

"Sorry, sir, we have to go," Scott told the politician.

We used a standard formation to evacuate the protectee back out to the vehicles. Thank God, both of our cars were still intact. If not, we might have had to commandeer a civilian mode of transport.

We got the principal secured, took up our positions in the vehicles, and sped out of there in record time. We did not stop for anything until we had the Serbian politician back at his house. No one asked any questions or hesitated. During our debriefing, we found out what had happened outside the campaign headquarters.

The Finn and the Brit had been sitting in their vehicles in front of the building, when the Finn spotted a subject approaching from the rear. Something about the guy seemed out of place. He was alone, for one thing, and appeared to be Albanian. Most of the people at this rally were Serbian and had traveled in groups. He was also walking in a stiff, robotic manner with his hands down by his sides.

The Finn alerted the Brit. Both jumped out of their vehicles and spun around with weapons in hand to get a bead on the Albanian. They yelled at the guy to stop right where he was and not advance any further. He kept walking toward them and was about thirty yards away.

It looked as if the subject dropped something and then bent down to pick it up. He was crossing through a row of parked cars between a Mercedes-Benz and a Toyota Corolla. It looked as if the object he dropped had rolled underneath the Mercedes.

Boom! The explosion came. It caused significant damage to that car as well as surrounding vehicles. Thank God, we were all okay. The Albanian had been carrying a grenade with the pin pulled, but his hand was still compressing the spoon. When he saw our protective detail, he got nervous and accidentally dropped the grenade, releasing the spoon. We believe he intended to walk into the campaign headquarters and take out as many Serbs as he could. Instead, by dropping his grenade and trying to pick it back up, he only blew

himself up. I don't like to say we were lucky that day; I like to say we were blessed. I don't believe in luck. I believe in the blessings of God.

No weapon formed against me shall prosper.

Prisoner Transport

Everyone on the team was given a nickname or call sign. The Brits had started referring to me as Cassie. Brits have a way of taking a one-syllable name or the first syllable of a name and putting a "y" or "ie" at the end of it. For example, our British team leader's surname was Clegg. Everyone called him Cleggy. Another guy on the team was named Jones. Yep, you guessed it. He was Jonesy. Now I was known as Cassie. I didn't necessarily care for it, but I didn't try to argue it either. I've heard worse nicknames.

Scott already had a call sign from when he worked on the Red Dog team in some of the most dangerous parts of south Atlanta. The Red Dogs would roll up in an unmarked van in the projects and would jump out of the van in the middle of a drug deal. Scott's call sign was "Southside." He might have been called Scotty, except for this one Scottish cop on the team. His last name was Walker, but everyone called him Scotty.

We were tasked with transporting a high-risk Serbian prisoner from the detention facility to his courtroom hearing. This guy had been some kind of high-level military official during the conflict and was accused of multiple human rights atrocities committed against Albanian civilians.

There were three of us on the transport team that day: Southside, Cleggy, and me. We drove an armored white Toyota Landcruiser with "UN" in big black letters on both sides, which stuck out like a sore thumb. On this type of high-risk detail, we normally would have had a follow car to provide rear security. There were no backup teams available for this detail, so we used a single vehicle. There was also a credible threat that this prisoner had friends who were going to try to bust him out. *Great. No better time to try to free your friend from*

custody than during a prisoner transport. Armored vehicles are not bullet-proof or bomb-proof, they are only resistant to those things. They're designed to buy you a few extra seconds if you ever find yourself on the *X* (site of an attack). Those few extra seconds may be just enough to save your life.

We showed up at the prison a little bit ahead of schedule, ready to get this detail over with. Cleggy was driving, so he waited outside in the car with the engine running. Southside and I went inside the prison to take custody of the prisoner. The conditions inside that Kosovo prison were so horrific, like nothing I'd ever seen. Just the smell nauseated me. It smelled like a zoo but worse. Dirtier. Old urine, feces, and blood stains covered the walls. I wanted to get in and out of there as quickly as we could. I looked over at Scott and could tell he was thinking the same.

They brought the Serbian out from the back. *If conditions in the intake room are this bad, I don't even want to imagine what goes on behind the scenes.* The guy was handcuffed with disposable plastic flex cuffs. His hands were cuffed in front of him, which I was not happy about, but I didn't say anything. It would be about a forty-five minute ride back to Pristina.

He was a large man, taller than I was, about the same height as Southside. He outweighed me by at least a hundred pounds. During the ride back, Cleggy drove, and Southside rode "shotgun" in the front passenger seat. The prisoner was sitting in the back left seat, behind Cleggy. I was in the back seat also, to the prisoner's right, behind Southside.

Cleggy was right-handed, so his sidearm was visible between the front seats. This Landcruiser did not have bench seats the way a typical prisoner transport vehicle would. It dawned on me once we were seated and had started rolling that this SUV was usually used for transporting VIP's. It had bucket seats with an arm rest between, the same as any luxury vehicle would. I should have realized it before.

Cleggy's pistol was visible and accessible to the back seat passengers. Not a good idea with the prisoner sitting right behind him. For about the first fifteen minutes of the drive, I kept looking at the prisoner to my left. Then I'd look down at Cleggy's pistol in its hol-

ster. The prisoner was not paying any attention to me; he just kept staring at Cleggy's pistol. Southside was sitting in the front passenger seat watching for outside threats, so he didn't have the same vantage point I had.

I'm not a mind reader, but I could tell the guy was thinking about reaching for Cleggy's gun. I started contingency planning. I imagined myself drawing my own pistol as soon as he made a move. I would put my gun to the side of his head and pull the trigger in order to stop the threat, if he forced my hand. My friends and I were going to go home at the end of this tour. In fact, my right hand was already on the grip of my Beretta. I had come a long way since ten years prior. I thought of the time I was a nineteen-year-old cadet at the Yacht Club, gripping a glass beer mug to smash over Maurice's head.

"Cleggy," I said.

"What's up, Cassie?"

"Pull the car over and stop please."

"What's up, Cassie?" he repeated. I could see Cleggy looking at me in the rearview mirror.

"Just do it please."

"All right, mate. Hang on." He pulled the car over and stopped.

"Scott, everything's okay. Just hang out here and keep an eye on our friend if you would be so kind. Cleggy and I need to step out for a sec," I said. When I met Cleggy around the back of the vehicle, I said, "The guy keeps eyeballing your gun like he wants it."

Cleggy was already taking his pistol out of the holster and securing it in the lock box in the trunk. I think he knew what this was about before I even said anything. We had worked together on so many details that we could often tell what the other was thinking. *Intuition.*

The rest of the transport went off without a hitch. The prisoner stood trial in Pristina and was found guilty. Years later, I was watching Fox News when a particular story caught my attention. That Serbian prisoner ended up killing himself in his cell at the Hague by swallowing a couple of cyanide capsules.

For you are from God and have overcome them, because the one who is in you, is greater than the one who is in the world.

Pink Knitted Booties

I was in an armored Toyota Landcruiser once again, sitting outside a courthouse in Pristina. My team was ready to transport this judge home and call it a day; it had been a long day. The month was August 2003. I had just been home on vacation during the Fourth of July. Kim and I had taken Nick on a wonderful Disney cruise around the Bahamas. I was daydreaming about my most recent time at home. I couldn't believe that I was now able to afford to take my family on nice vacations. *We never would have been able to afford that on my CPD salary.*

Scott was working a different detail that day. In fact, the unit chief had split us up, so we didn't get to work together much anymore. I mostly worked with Team Echo now, and Scott mostly worked with Team Charlie. They didn't want too many Americans on one team for diversity's sake. American and British contingents made up the largest numbers in theatre. Stacking a special ops team disproportionately with "Yanks and Brits" would have been easy.

My driver was an American guy named Al who was relatively new to the mission. He was a cop from Alabama and had only been in Kosovo for about four months. Al could tell I was drifting, mentally and emotionally. Another officer named Keith from the Police Service of Northern Ireland was roving the area on foot. We also had a Norwegian female officer, Kari, on the team now. She was posted inside the courthouse, close to the judge's office.

My mind raced back and forth between memories of my most recent time at home and stories Keith had told me about Belfast. I have the utmost respect for the guys who belong to the Royal Ulster Constabulary (RUC). They've sustained decades of attacks from the IRA (Irish Republican Army). Many Americans nowadays have for-

gotten about that struggle, but I haven't forgotten. *Such a great time I had with my wife and son back home. So many RUC brothers lost to IRA attackers. Could we be attacked like that here today?*

"John," I heard Al say. I actually appreciated the break in silence. "You okay? What are you thinking about?"

"Aw, nothing," I said. "Just remembering my time at home, that's all. Daydreaming."

"You're getting close to the end of your two years here," he reminded me. "You'll be home soon. You gonna try to come back for another mission?"

"I don't think so. I'm ready to go home and stay home for a while." *Short-timer's attitude.*

As we sat there chatting, an old Roma Gypsy woman approached us on my side of the vehicle. We'd grown accustomed to homeless people and beggars coming up to our cars. We would typically shoo them away. At first, this lady seemed like such a person.

She walked up to my window, and I could tell she was carrying something in each hand. She came closer. She held up a pair of pink knitted baby booties with her right hand and dangled them in front of my face. I looked down at her other hand, which she kept held down by her side. Her left hand held a pair of blue knitted booties.

She kept shaking the pink booties and pointing at me. Without giving it a second thought, I shooed her away. She finally walked away, rounded the corner, and disappeared. This whole exchange lasted less than a minute. Al was laughing the whole time.

Not two minutes after the old Gypsy woman walked away, my cell phone rang. I pulled it out of my pocket. It was Kim.

"Are you ready to be a daddy again?"

I sat silent for a moment and then replied with, "It's a girl, babe. It's a girl this time. I don't know how, but I just know it. I gotta go. I'll call you back."

I told Al I was getting out of the car for a few minutes. I jumped out and ran up and down the street. I rounded the corners looking for the Roma lady, but I did not want to wander too far from my detail either. I didn't see her. I walked back to the car, disappointed.

"Al, did you just see an old lady shaking a pair of pink baby booties at me?" *Maybe I just imagined it.*

"Yeah. I saw her too. Just as sure as I'm sitting here. And that phone call was about your wife being pregnant, wasn't it?"

One of my few regrets in life is that I did not buy those pink knitted booties from that old woman. It's one of the strangest things that's ever happened to me, and I wish I had the booties as a keepsake. Our daughter, Alex, is fourteen years old now.

Thirtieth Birthday Dinner

It was the end of September 2003. I had turned twenty-nine and thirty in Kosovo, but God willing, I would not turn thirty-one there. I would be home for my thirty-first birthday on October 8. It had been a good two-year tour, but I was really ready to go home. I'd gained a lot of valuable real-world experience and made many new friends—the kind of friends you stay in touch with forever.

I'd celebrated my twenty-ninth birthday by driving out to the US Army base at Camp Bondsteel, about a forty-minute drive from Pristina. I didn't tell anyone I was going. I just jumped into one of the extra Toyota 4Runners and went. No one even knew it was my birthday; I just wanted to disappear for a few hours.

We were civilian police, not military, but all any of us had to do was show a UN Police badge and an American passport at the front gate at Bondsteel, and we were in. We had full access to the gym and medical facilities as well as the Post Exchange (PX). American officers tried to keep Bondsteel runs on the down-low. All the internationals knew that the Americans had the biggest and best PX in Kosovo. Whenever they found out we were making a Bondsteel run, they always wanted to go with us or would give us long lists of items to bring back. Bondsteel was the only place in country where one could get a Burger King Whopper. I celebrated my twenty-ninth birthday by treating myself to a Whopper and onion rings. It may sound like a sad birthday dinner, but at the time, it meant a lot to me.

I'd spent my thirtieth birthday with a group of new coworker/ friends who took me out to one of the Serbian villages for a traditional Serbian dinner. The hosts served us huge platters of grilled meat and vegetables. They also brought out a beautiful chopped salad, over-flowing with cucumber, tomato, goat cheese, and Greek olives. In the

middle of the table, there was a big bowl of fresh *ayvar*, a sweet-and-spicy roasted red pepper relish typically served with Balkan dishes. I wasn't quite sure what to put the *ayvar* on, so I put it on everything. This was a celebratory feast. We all ate way too much, yet the hosts just kept bringing out more food.

I had to work a detail the next morning, so I couldn't have too much to drink. However, it was traditional to drink a shot of *slivovitz* at the end of the meal, so I knew they were bringing it out sooner or later. *Slivovitz* is a plum brandy popular in Eastern Europe and is also known as *rakia*. Some of the Americans called it "rocket fuel." It was strong but also delicious. We had two rounds of *slivovitz* shots. It was my thirtieth birthday party after all, plus the brandy would help digest all of the food we'd just consumed.

On the wall behind us hung a large framed picture of Slobodan Milosevic, which I found a bit unsettling. Most of the Kosovo Albanians celebrated Bill Clinton as a hero for helping them gain their independence from Serbia. The Serbs obviously did not share the sentiment. My hope was that they had not poisoned our food.

We were five Americans, two Bulgarians, two Brits, a Romanian, and a French guy. The Bulgarians and the Romanian shared a common language with the Serbian restaurant owners, so they were able to communicate with each other, which put me more at ease. I hoped they were telling them that Americans do not have anything against Serbs and we were not there to cause any trouble. We were only there to have a nice evening and spend money. Money seems to be the universal language.

I had noticed that the majority of Bulgarian and Romanian police officers chose to rent accommodations in Serbian villages. Most of them did not like the Albanians and felt that Bill Clinton had done Serbia a huge disservice by stepping into their conflict. I tried to stay away from the politics and cultural dynamics. I was there to do a job and then get back home to my family. However, I will say this: I am of the opinion that Bill Clinton mainly intervened in the Serbian-Albanian conflict in order to divert the media spotlight off his Monica Lewinsky scandal. I find the timing of the US stepping into that conflict suspicious. Washington spin doctors and

the news media have a way of getting the tail to wag the dog. *It's an old magician's trick...smoke and mirrors...sleight of hand. "Watch what this hand is doing; don't pay any attention to this other hand."*

Toward the end of the evening, a large middle-aged Serbian man walked into the restaurant. He took a look around, and his eyes settled right on our table. One of my American friends was a big African-American guy; his name was also John. Whenever the two of us hung out together, people called us Big John and Little John.

The Serbian man walked straight over to our table and stood right behind Big John. He put both of his hands on Big John's shoulders and started massaging them. Then he leaned down and started speaking in Serbian into Big John's ear. The Bulgarians and the Romanian probably knew what the guy was saying, but they wouldn't tell us. They just laughed. This went on for about a full minute before the Serb finally walked away.

To lighten the mood, one of the other American officers, Eric, said, "I happen to speak and understand a little bit of Serbo-Croatian from the time I spent in Bosnia. I believe he just said that he has always fantasized about making love to a large black man."

Everyone at our table busted out laughing. It was a while before we regained our composure enough to pay the bill and go.

I've enjoyed this evening and will look back on it as a fond memory from my time in Kosovo, but God willing, I will be home with my wife and son for my thirty-first birthday.

New Contract

I flew home on October 1, 2003. It was the beginning of the new fiscal year for the government. Big changes always seem to happen around October. I was happy to be heading home in one piece. I needed a break from the Albanians, and I believe they were starting to feel the same way about the international peacekeepers.

The week before I left, there had been a violent protest in front of UN police headquarters in downtown Pristina. A large group of Albanian civilians was protesting the presence of an international police force. They felt as if they were capable of policing themselves and wanted the IPTF out. It started out as peaceful but quickly turned violent as they began throwing bricks and bottles at us. I was there in full riot gear, complete with helmet, shield, and long stick. Several officers and many civilians were injured. Just when I thought the protest was about to escalate into a full-blown riot, the Jordanian SPU (Special Police Unit) rolled up in big armored trucks and started hosing the crowd down with pepper spray. That sent the Albanian protestors scrambling. *Thank God for the Jords.*

I would be thirty-one in less than a week. In the months leading up to my end of mission in Kosovo, I had been sending out resumes to different security contracting companies. I wanted to be home with my wife and son for the holidays and also for the birth of our daughter in March. I also knew that our savings would run out after six months, and I would need to get back to work by April.

Many of my American teammates from Kosovo, including Southside Scott, had found jobs with a private military corporation called Blackwater (BW). That company had been awarded the State Department contract to provide a protective security detail for Paul

Bremer in Baghdad. Bremer was appointed special envoy for the Coalition Provisional Authority in Iraq.

Right after the United States took Saddam Hussein out of power in April of 2003, President Bush had to appoint an American leader to run that country until it was stable enough to hold its own democratic process. Bremer was the man for the job. It would be very dangerous, and BW was hiring guys who had experience working high-threat protective details, just like the ones we'd worked in Kosovo. They weren't just hiring former military guys anymore; they opened up the contract to ex-cops, like me.

Blackwater had also been awarded a DEA contract in Afghanistan. I don't think that was a protection contract though. I believe it had something to do with the eradication of poppy fields. I didn't care what they put me to work doing; I was just ready to get back to work.

The Lord is my light and my salvation. Whom shall I fear? The Lord is the stronghold of my life. Of whom shall I be afraid?

Meanwhile back at home, Kim's obstetrician had Alex's estimated due date way off because she was going by the date of Kim's last menstrual cycle. We told the doctor early on that Kim's cycles had always been irregular. Sometimes she could just skip a month or have two in the same month.

Because we knew the exact dates I'd been home during my CTO from Kosovo, and we had the exact dates of our Fourth of July vacation in the Bahamas, Kim had a high degree of certainty about our date of conception. The obstetrician would not listen and insisted that she use her silly chart for estimation, based on the dates of Kim's last cycle. *Whatever.*

They call it the "medical practice" for a reason. They're still practicing. It's very good, but it's not perfect. Most times they get it right, but sometimes they get it wrong. It's not called "medical perfection."

The AFP (alpha-fetoprotein) test is supposed to be run between the sixteenth and eighteenth week of pregnancy. Kim's obstetrician ran it during, what she guesstimated, was the sixteenth week. According to Kim's calculations, Alex was only in her twelfth week

of development. We expected the protein count to come back low. According to science and medicine though, a low protein reading can indicate a whole host of genetic disorders, to include Down syndrome.

The doctor was adamant; there was a good chance Alex would be born with Down's. She even offered us the option of terminating the pregnancy, as it was still early enough to do so. Another option was we could wait and do an amniocentesis within a couple of weeks, which would show us more definitively if Alex had Down's. However, by then, we may have been too late to terminate. We were right on the cusp.

For Kim and I, there was no decision to be made. We didn't even really need to talk it over. We both knew in our hearts that we were keeping our daughter. She would be beautiful and wonderful, and we would love her no matter what. We went through with the amnio just to give us some peace of mind. The results came back negative for any disorders.

For you formed my inward parts; you knitted me together in my mother's womb. I praise you; for I am fearfully and wonderfully made. Wonderful are your works, my soul knows it very well.

Alex was born in March of 2004, weeks after the doctor's guess-timated due date. The date Kim had guessed was very close to accurate, within a couple of days. Alex was born free of any genetic disorders and at a normal birth weight. Sometimes doctors should listen to their patients.

The labor and delivery went really fast, as if our baby girl was ready to be in this world. The nurses told Kim to stop pushing and wait for the obstetrician to get there. Kim said, "I stopped pushing a while ago. She's coming, whether y'all are ready for her or not."

Alex was born into the hands of one of the nurses before the doctor ever arrived. She never even cried; she just opened her beautiful brown eyes and looked around the room.

Oh God, she is perfect. Thank you again, oh Lord, for your many blessings.

A New Mission

I stayed home for exactly one month after Alex's birth, just to make sure Kim was back on her feet. My new contract deployment would be sending me to the south central region of Asia in May of 2004. I didn't know exactly where. When they told me the region, I figured somewhere in either Afghanistan or Pakistan. I thought they were sending me out there to help find Bin Laden or something.

I just wanted to be a part of the mission; I didn't care where they were sending me or what I'd be doing. I would have gone wherever and done whatever. A good friend of mine who used to be an FBI agent (I'll call him Chase) told me something very wise when I first went to work for the USG.

Chase said, "John, no matter how much we love Uncle Sam, he ain't ever gonna love us back. We're his little expendables. It don't matter which branch we work for: FBI, DOS (Department of State), DOD (Department of Defense), IC (Intelligence Community), DEA (Drug Enforcement Administration), or whichever acronym owns the contract. It's all the same to Uncle Sam. He doesn't care about you or me. Don't try to stay in this line of work for the long haul. Carve out your little slice and then get out while you're still young. If you keep chasing the bullet, eventually you're gonna catch the bullet."

I didn't want to believe him when he made that statement, but it turned out to be quite true. I tried to keep my focus on the big mission and not just what was going on with me. It was the best I could do as a low man on the totem pole. *Too many chiefs and not enough Indians; I just want to be a good Indian.* That was the attitude I tried to maintain.

People making small talk would ask me what I did for a living. I've used my same standard reply since 2001, when I worked my first DynCorp contract. I never saw any need to change my answer: *I'm an international police advisor for the State Department.* One of the officers I worked with in Kosovo was from the Czech Republic; we called him "Chekov." He used to say, with his Eastern European accent, "Cassie is kind of quiet, like the quiet kid in the sandbox. I think he really works for the IG (Inspector General) office, and he's spying on us."

My security clearance finally came through, so I reached out to Southside. I wanted to know where he was working now and if there was a chance we might get to work together again. His security clearance had come through also, but well before mine. He was deployed to the Middle East, assigned to one of the teams of people tasked with finding weapons of mass destruction (WMDs).

This is a side note, and it's just my personal opinion: I have never seen, heard, or read anything official about whether we found WMDs in Iraq or not. My opinion is that Saddam Hussein did have them. More specifically, he had chemical weapons. He'd already demonstrated in 1987, when he unleashed mustard gas and nerve agents against the Kurdish people of northern Iraq; he had the ability, opportunity, and intent to use WMDs. I believe he moved them into neighboring Syria, prior to the United States' arrival in Iraq in 2003. They are the same chemical weapons Bashar Assad used against his own people ten years later. It's a matter of simple math if you put two and two together. If Saddam didn't have anything to hide, then why would he not cooperate with UN weapons inspectors? Our news media and certain politicians will try to convince us that President Bush was not justified in going into Iraq because there were no WMDs. I will always believe the weapons were in Syria while we were looking for them in Iraq. *It's an old magician's trick... the shell game.*

Southside told me in an e-mail that he was happy with his decision to work for BW. He said everything was going well, and it seemed like a good company to work for. The man who owned the company, Erik Prince, was a good Christian. Right after I finished

reading Scott's e-mail, I turned on Fox News. It was March 31, 2004. The big news of the day was about the "Fallujah Four."

Stephen Helvenston, Jerry Zovko, Wesley Batalona, and Michael Teague were the four Blackwater contractors who were killed with grenades and small-arms fire while escorting a food and supply shipment through Fallujah, Iraq. Their bodies were dragged from the vehicle they were riding only to be beaten, burned, mutilated, and hung over the bridge that crosses the Euphrates River. The locals responsible for their deaths filmed it and cheered as they committed those atrocities. The graphic footage was shown by the news media over and over. I still can't get those images out of my head. It made me want to go work for BW even more. I wanted some justice… some payback.

Put your sword back into its place. For all who take up the sword will surely perish by the sword. But how then shall the Scriptures be fulfilled?

Blackwater

Prior to my first BW deployment, I spent most of April 2004 at their training facility in Moyock, North Carolina. It was another training and vetting course similar to what I had experienced at the Crucible in 2001. This was more intense though and was longer in duration. The stakes and standards were higher. Guys were being dropped from the course like flies this time, which was discouraging. Some of them seemed like good dudes, but they just made too many critical errors. The BW evaluators were extremely scrutinous and particular. I barely passed the course, but I did it.

Somehow, I believe by the grace of God, I was able to show the evaluators what they wanted to see. The shooting scores had to be higher on the range, and the shooting times were much shorter than what I was used to from Kosovo. I was reminded of the line from the movie <u>Young Guns</u>: *"We're Regulators. We regulate any stealing of this property. We're damn good too. But you can't be any geek off the street. Gotta be handy with the steel if you know what I mean, earn your keep."*

Blackwater had the best shooting facilities I had ever seen. My favorite was the range where we shot from the open doors and windows of a wooden structure that resembled a house. The targets were round steel "pie plates," which would pop up for a few seconds, then pop back down randomly. It was like playing Whac-a-Mole with guns. The targets ranged from seven meters to twenty-five meters away, and you had to get a certain number of hits to pass.

They also ran us through various shoot/don't shoot scenarios inside a state-of-the-art "kill house." If you flagged too many friendlies, or had a negligent discharge with a simulation round, you were gone. This was serious business, and I felt as if I was being groomed

for something really important, even more important than the work we were doing in Kosovo.

I only had one security violation during the whole course. I still say that I did not do what the instructor said I did though. He was watching us from above on the catwalk and said I flagged my partner. "Flagging" means I swept my loaded weapon across my partner's back.

It's called "close quarters battle" (CQB) for a reason. I may have come close, but I know I didn't do it. I don't think the instructor had the best vantage point above us. I still say I did not flag anyone, but it didn't do any good to argue with an instructor. I have always been very much aware of my muzzle discipline, as well as my trigger finger discipline, but they were bouncing guys from the course and sending them home left and right. I learned early on that it was best to pick my battles carefully. I rogered up, accepted my security violation, and swore I would do better on the next run.

There was Hogan's Alley, where the instructors and role players simulated attacks on our convoys. The instructors had remote kill switches for our car engines, and we would be expected to evacuate the vehicles when they suddenly "died." What they were looking for was for us to do something to get off the X. We had to get our team and protectee out of the kill zone using whatever means necessary to stay alive, even if it meant getting shot up a little bit. They put us in no-win situations sometimes, and we couldn't just freeze up. We had to keep moving, no matter what.

They even had a vehicle rollover simulator. They would flip us upside down, and we would have to evacuate the vehicle. It was tough. Tougher than anything I had experienced. My adrenaline was pumping so much at times that I didn't even realize I was being pelted with paintballs and sim rounds. Later, after I was back in my room showering, I could see where I was covered with bruises, welts, and broken skin. *Look at me. I'm a mess.* I still have scars from some of the simulation hits, where they dug in deep enough and bled. *They're especially painful when training in cold weather, and the paintballs and sims are frozen from being stored outside. Yay! Fun!*

There was more physical training, both conditioning and punitive. If any of us made a mistake, we would have to suck it up and do whatever the instructors told us to do. I was embracing the suck again. I wanted to be a PMC (private military contractor). I felt really privileged and honored to be there. By the time we got to the last part of the training, the hand-to-hand combat scenarios, I was exhausted. Advil, Tiger Balm, Ace bandages and braces, and Rockstar energy drinks became my best friends.

The evaluators would put us in a dimly lit room with blacked-out hoods over our heads. Wearing the hood, I couldn't see a thing, but I could hear people moving around me, getting set up. I tried not to let it upset me. Instead, I tried to use the sound of movement to know what to expect when the hood came off. Once it came off, we had to react to whatever scenario we were presented with. Some scenarios required no action. For example, it might just be a person standing in front of you, asking for directions. Others required us to fight with role players who were dressed in protective outfits. The outfits were to protect them when we started striking them.

I fought so much and so hard during the fight scenarios that by the time the last scenario came around, I couldn't even lift my arms to defend myself properly. My attacker gave me a cupped-hand slap to my left ear, which made me angry. I wasn't wearing any protective gear and had already sustained some hearing loss because my left earplug had fallen out during a shoot and move scenario on the firing range. I was dazed, and my ear was ringing. I tackled the role player, straddled him, and started punching him full force in his head and face with both my fists. He was wearing a protective helmet and face mask, so all I was really doing was hurting my own knuckles.

"*Endex!*" the instructors yelled. This meant it was the end of the exercise. "You can't do that to the role players!"

"Well, what else was I supposed to do?" I yelled back. "The guy popped my eardrum! That's what I would have done in real life! These scenarios are all canned BS!"

I was starting to develop an attitude. I had endured about as much abuse as I could take. I gathered my senses, said a short prayer for peace, and helped the role player up off the floor. He and I shook

hands, saying there were no hard feelings. He stumbled out of the room, dazed by the strikes I had administered to his helmet. I hoped he was okay.

I took a butt-chewing from the instructors for "viciously attacking" one of the role players, but they must have seen something in me they liked because I passed the course.

The beatings will continue until morale improves.

A New Call Sign

I sat in my hotel room at the Islamabad Marriott; I'd never been to Pakistan before. There would be a two-day layover in this hotel, before I could catch the onward flight to the forward operating base (FOB) in Afghanistan. I was going to use the layover days to try beating the jet lag. It had been a long flight from the States, and there was a huge time difference. My days and nights were mixed up, and once I got to the work site, I wanted to be good to go. My body wanted to sleep all day, but at night, I couldn't fall asleep. I walked around the hotel in kind of a fog the whole first day.

I tried to nap during the day, but the hotel staff kept knocking on my door, bringing trays of fruit, tea, and snacks. They knocked on my door about once every hour to see if I needed anything. *Weird.* At one point, I thought maybe they were trying to keep tabs on me because I was an American. I finally figured out that if I put the "Do Not Disturb" sign on my door, they'd stop bothering me.

I looked around the room and noticed some distinctive indicators that I was in a Muslim country. On top of the dresser was a round sticker, about the size of a drink coaster. It had a picture of the *Kaaba* on it. It's the big black cube Muslims walk around when they make the hajj pilgrimage to their holy city of Mecca, in Saudi Arabia. The sticker also had an arrow, which pointed toward Mecca so the room guests would know which way to face when they prayed to Allah. There was also a copy of the Koran on top of the dresser. As a Christian, I did not find these things particularly useful, yet I appreciated the religious sentiment.

The room had a minibar, but it contained only soda and sparkling water. On top of the mini fridge was a cocktail menu. Any non-Muslim westerner was allowed to call the room service number

and order a beer or cocktail, but once the drink was delivered to the room, a Western passport would have to be shown. Also, the room occupant would have to sign a waiver declaring to be a non-Muslim. The instructions on the menu were very clear, and they were written in several different languages. I had made up my mind that I was not going to drink while overseas. I wanted to maintain 100 percent of my situational awareness at all times, and I couldn't do it if I was even the slightest bit impaired.

I turned on the television to watch some world news and was able to find the English-speaking version of Al Jazeera. The station was airing unedited footage of an American named Nicholas Berg, dressed in an orange jumpsuit.

The video starts with him sitting on the floor in front of five Islamist militants, all dressed in black. The militants are wearing hoods and ski masks so you can't see their faces. One reads a letter out loud, stating that this American will have to pay the price for the mistreatment of Muslim prisoners at Guantanamo Bay. Two of the militants proceed to hold Berg down, while another savagely beheads him with a knife. In the video, Berg can be heard screaming as the militants chant, "*Allahu Akbar*" ("God is great"). One of the men holds the severed head in front of the camera and then lays it on top of Berg's body. *That's not the work of God.*

I couldn't sleep after watching that, so I walked downstairs to the lobby and ate breakfast. I made myself a beautiful plate of food from the breakfast buffet, and as I sat there eating it, I made myself a silent promise. *They'll never take me alive.* It was evident to me that if I were taken alive, very bad things would happen. I never want to be on CNN or Fox or Al Jazeera in an orange jumpsuit, begging for my life, only to have my head cut off. I'd rather control my own fate.

Suicide is frowned upon in the Bible. It's not what God wants for us; I have strong feelings about that. When I was a little kid, my Aunt Fran shot herself in the chest with a pistol because she struggled with depression and was in an abusive relationship. Twenty years later, her son, my cousin Mickey, killed himself the same way. I'll never fully understand their reasons, but I know I miss them dearly and wish they were still here. Unfortunately, I've also lost a few

friends and coworkers to suicide over the years. *I wish they'd called me, or called someone, to talk about things and ask for help. Instead, they found a permanent solution to a temporary problem.*

However, I also believe there are exceptions. Being taken prisoner in a *jihad* is one of those exceptions. I promised myself I would fight as hard as I could and take out as many of the threats as I could, but if we were being overrun and there was no way to win, I would save my last bullet for myself. For most regular people with normal jobs, that seems scary to think about, but I've talked to many of my coworkers who have made themselves the same promise. How many American prisoners of war have been captured and then eventually released alive in this global war against terrorism? Not many, as far as I know. Not like in previous wars. The odds aren't good. I think God would understand if I chose to take my own life in that situation. As long as I'm doing what I believe is right, I also believe God will take care of me. This doesn't necessarily mean I will live. It just means I get to go to Heaven when it's all said and done.

I stepped off the back of the C-130 onto the tarmac a couple days later. It was scheduled to drop off a bunch of supplies, as well as transfer a few personnel, between the major hub I'd just left and this remote site. The heat was the first thing I noticed. It was at least 120 degrees.

I helped to unload cargo and luggage off of the bird and then helped load it onto pickup trucks. I watched the guys who were leaving, shaking hands and giving hugs goodbye, but I didn't know any of them. They were heading home. I helped them load their luggage onto the bird before jumping into one of the pickup trucks headed back to base.

The trucks dropped us new arrivals off in front of the tactical operations center (TOC) where we unloaded our luggage. A large, bald, old, salty cuss with a Monopoly Man mustache stepped out of the TOC to greet us. His name was Hershel, call sign "MC" (Master Chief). I recognized him from several documentaries I'd seen on the History Channel about old-school Navy SEALs. The man is a legend in the SEAL community.

The MC gave each of us a firm handshake as well as a bro hug/ back slap. He was wearing a brown short-sleeved Under Armour T-shirt. It smelled as if he had not washed that shirt in a while, and I wondered about regular showers here. He had a strong smell of man musk, which I figured I'd have to get used to. This was an austere, expeditionary environment, the likes of which I had never experienced. He introduced himself politely, welcomed us to the base, and asked us to step inside the TOC.

The MC looked through our passports. They were in alphabetical order by last name. Mine was first: "John Nicholas Cassel, who is that?" he asked in a booming voice.

I raised my hand. "That's me, Master Chief."

"Do you have a call sign?"

We were all Americans at this base, and I never particularly cared for "Cassie," so I replied, "No, Master Chief. I don't have one."

"Well, we'll come up with one for you soon enough," he said. "What's your background?"

I told him about my previous experience in a concise manner, and he seemed (somewhat) impressed. He liked former law-enforcement types. I felt as if I was going to fit in here, kind of like a misfit on the Island of Misfit Toys.

Later, I followed the crowd to eat dinner in the GP (general purpose) tent. I sat down in the chow hall, in front of my tray of food, and felt thankful for it. I bowed my head to pray over my meal. The Master Chief walked into the chow hall tent just then. He waited until I finished praying. Then, in that booming voice of his, he said, "Are you Catholic?"

I looked up at him, then looked around. The other guys were watching. I told him, "Well, MC, I used to be Catholic, but I haven't claimed that particular religion in a while. I am a Christian. I do believe in Jesus Christ as my Savior."

Hershel hunkered over me and said, "Yeah, I used to be Catholic too. Once they baptize you, you're screwed. It's not going to help you out here, son. You think being a Christian will save you? It won't. You're going to die out here, just like the rest of us. Two pieces of

advice: don't ever drink with the client, and don't ever try to screw the client. Hell, I think you're a saint. I'm gonna call you St. Nick."

I will never forget him saying that to me, just like that. My call sign has been St. Nick ever since, and it was just because he had seen my middle name on my passport and then saw me praying over my food in the chow hall. The more I thought about it, the more it seemed like a fitting call sign for me.

My son's name is also Nicholas. I had just seen a young man named Nicholas Berg savagely executed on television by Islamist militants. Christmas has always been my favorite holiday and many of my family and friends call me "Holiday John" because I get so into celebrating Christmas. I had done some historical research on the real Saint Nicholas (not the fictional Santa Claus but the historical Saint Nick).

Because of the many miracles attributed to him, he's sometimes referred to as "Nikolaos the Wonderworker." He came from an area of Asia Minor, which in the fourth century was considered Greece but is now part of Turkey. My ancestors came from Malta, close to that region. He was not a big, fat, jolly guy, but he did have a beard. You can find many historically accurate paintings and drawings of him floating around on the internet. He is the patron saint of sailors, merchants, archers, repentant thieves, children, brewers, pawnbrokers, students, and travelers. His reputation revolved around his habit of secret gift giving. This gave rise to the fictional character of Santa Claus. Also, Saint Nicholas Day is still celebrated on the sixth of December throughout much of Eastern Europe, in the Orthodox Christian religion. December 6 just happens to be my mom's birthday. For all these reasons, I decided "St. Nick" was a good call sign for me. I decided to keep it.

People come up to me even now and say, "Saint Nick! Santa Claus! Did you bring us gifts? Did you get your call sign because of the beard?"

I like to keep things simple. Only in this memoir do I explain the full reasons I'm known to the security contracting world as St. Nick. I usually reply with, "Yep. You got it. That's it." In my mind, as an afterthought, I smile and think, *But there's so much more to the story.*

The "Alamo"

Two days after I left the Marriott in Islamabad, a suicide operative wearing a bomb vest walked into the lobby of the same hotel during breakfast and blew himself up, injuring and killing dozens of people. It was yet another blessing from God that I was not sitting there eating breakfast near the lobby when it happened. I've had a few close brushes like that over the course of my career.

I adapted quickly to life on the compound. I didn't have much choice. It was either adapt and overcome or go home. Most of the guys I worked with there had served in the military and spent time in the field, so they knew what it was like to rough it. A few guys showed up, then voluntarily went home short-of-tour once they saw what the living conditions were like.

The most rugged living conditions I had been through prior to this were the two years I spent "urban camping" as a cop in Kosovo. If you want to know what that's like, wait until the middle of winter, then switch off the main breaker of your house for three days so you have no power. Also, make sure the gas is off so you have no heat and no hot water. While you're at it, turn off the main water valve and get by with bottled water to drink, bathe, wash dishes, and flush the toilet. Remember, it's winter, so let's hope your pipes aren't frozen. Get yourself a small generator, a kerosene heater, and keep a stash of candles on hand. Then for one day, turn all your utilities back on just to remind yourself how nice it was to have all that. Then turn it all back off again for three days. That's what it was like. I'm talking about a bitter Siberian-style winter.

This new work site in south central Asia represented a new style of roughing it for me. The most disenchanting part to me was most

of the new skills I'd learned back at BW would not be put to use here. This was a base overwatch position and did not require us to go outside the wire. There was really nowhere for us to go if we did leave the wire, as we were in the middle of the desert. We were there to make sure the base remained functional and did not get overrun by bad guys. I adopted the attitude that I was getting paid a healthy daily rate to be there, so I needed to do the best job I could, even if I was just filling sandbags or fortifying fighting positions.

It reminded me of a scene from the *Wild West*. In the middle of the camp, there stood a limestone building with a domed roof. It looked very much like the Alamo. In fact, that's what we affectionately called it. I just prayed that my time there would not end like the Battle of the Alamo.

As a pep talk and to remind us how important our mission was, every few days or so, Master Chief Hershel would gather the security team together near OP (overwatch position) number 2. I soon figured out he gathered us there because it was far down the airfield, away from the eyes and ears of the USG staffers and military personnel. His pep talks usually consisted of telling us, "This base is going to be overrun by tangos (terrorists) soon! You might as well get it through your mainspring housing group right now!" He was using a gun-part analogy, but of course, we all knew what he meant.

He would tell us, "Gentlemen! Enjoy these plush accommodations while you have them! If you live through this, you will have fond memories that you may be able to tell your grandkids about someday! If you don't have the warrior mentality, then you are going to die out here! Not me! I'm going to live to be a thousand years old!"

We would all cheer. The MC's pep talks were motivating, but they got old after a while. The base never got attacked. The Master Chief was just trying to keep us in a certain mindset.

I slept on a cot in a tent, showered in an outdoor stall, and used outhouses to take care of business. Every squad had extra duties which would rotate from week to week. Those duties ranged from collecting trash from the cans, to collecting poop and pee bins from the outhouses and burning them with diesel fuel in a burn pit, and to washing dishes, pots, and pans on KP (kitchen patrol). It wasn't what

I expected to be doing, but I got used to it. I understood I was the low man on the totem pole. I had to earn my keep, even if it meant serving on "poop burn duty," as we called it.

Let us hold tightly without wavering to the hope we affirm, for God can be trusted to keep His promise.

Camel Spiders

I had never seen a camel spider before. They're very ugly and range from the size of a half dollar to the size of your hand. They're tan and hairy, and they are venomous. If they bite you, you won't die, but you can get very sick. The camel spider is in the arachnid family, but is neither a spider nor a scorpion. It's something in between, and I found them to be quite aggressive and just nasty, I would have left them alone, if they'd left me alone.

I had gotten into the habit of banging my boots out onto the floor before putting them on. We were allowed to wear shorts during our shifts because the temp got up to 120 degrees most days. I had taken to shaving my body, face, and head so that I didn't have extra hair to hold in heat. I wore sunglasses all day and clear goggles in the evening, for when the sandstorms blew in. The sand was like moon dust and it got into absolutely everything; the winds made sure of it. I kept a scarf around my neck to pull over my mouth and nose, so as not to breathe in the sand when it started blowing around.

I had heard a story about a guy putting his boots on in a hurry without banging them out on the floor. He received a nice scorpion sting on the side of his foot in exchange for his rush effort. He went on his shift, but his foot swelled so much he had to cut his boot off with his pocketknife. This particular evening, I was glad I had gotten into the habit of banging my boots out, like the cowboys in the Wild West used to. A black scorpion, about the size of a half-dollar, came scurrying out of my right boot. I quickly dispatched him with both soles of my stylish footwear, like alternating twin sledgehammers.

I had heard guys tell stories about snakes they had seen on base, but I never saw any. I did see what looked like big snake tracks in the sand, but I never laid eyes on any actual snakes. Some of the tracks in

the sand were very long and wide. They ran from the outskirts of the camp to right underneath our tents. Once, I got up in the middle of the night and stepped out of my cot. It felt as if my left foot might have touched one that was sleeping underneath my tent floor. It slithered away quickly and scared the heck out of me. I later researched the types of snakes native to that region. The native species included vipers and cobras. *Nice. The only good snake, in my opinion, is a dead snake. I don't really care whether it's venomous or nonvenomous.*

When I was on the midnight shift on top of the Alamo, I felt like the king of the world. I could look all around the camp through the forward-looking infrared (FLIR) camera and see for miles in the dark. The FLIR could switch between night vision and thermal-image mode. I was looking for bad guys trying to sneak into our camp, but I usually only saw desert foxes trying to catch some food. Motion sensors set up around the camp's perimeter would go off every once in a while, usually set off by some wild animal. I could see them through the FLIR.

One early morning, while it was still pitch-black outside, another contractor came to relieve me from my post on top of the Alamo.

"Hey, Jay. Where are you from back home?" I asked, just trying to make some small talk.

"Virginia Beach," he replied. "Funny story, I went to high school in Virginia Beach with this black kid. He was always getting in trouble for not paying attention during class. He was always writing down song lyrics. That black kid was Pharrell Williams. Can you imagine that? I wish I'd written down some of those song lyrics with him and paid less attention in school."

"Nice," I replied. "It's too bad you aren't still in touch with him. I visited Virginia Beach once. If I ever get back there, I'm gonna try to get on the 700 Club and talk to Pat Robertson about working out here." We laughed.

I wished Jay a nice, quiet shift. I had a load of laundry ready to be pulled out of the dryer in the laundry tent, so I was eager to go downstairs and get it. It's funny how small personal tasks like that became so important in that environment. As I was descending the

outside staircase, I switched on my red headlamp so I could see the stairs in front of me. (During hours of darkness, we were not allowed to turn on any white light, only red lens-filtered light. White light can be spotted from much farther away than red. Also, white light ruins your night-vision capabilities; red light doesn't.)

On one part of the staircase, I had to walk underneath an overhead structure and felt something drop onto the back of my neck. I instinctively brushed it away with my right hand. I couldn't see it, but I knew it was a camel spider. It felt about the same size as my hand, and it was hairy. I couldn't see where it went after I brushed it off, so I picked up my walking pace. It had not bitten me, so I figured I was okay.

I stopped by my tent to drop my gear. I took my boots off and put some flip-flops on, then walked to the laundry tent to retrieve my clean clothes. It was only about a thirty-foot walk, and I was still using my red lens headlamp to see in front of me. The winds had started to pick up and sand was blowing around me. I stepped into the laundry tent which was dimly lit by a small white light. I switched off my headlamp.

As I stepped toward the dryer, a camel spider about the size of my hand came running out from underneath and then stopped. He was on the floor of the tent about six feet from me and raised his antennae to study me. I stopped, thinking that if I didn't mess with him he would go away. We studied each other for a few seconds, then he charged toward my feet.

Am I in Hell right now? Is this the same camel spider that dropped down onto my neck at the Alamo? Or one of his friends maybe? Are they communicating with one another?

I stomped him with my flip-flopped right foot and held it there for a minute. Stomping him felt so good that I even twisted my foot from side to side to hear the crunch. Then I lifted my foot and looked at him. His body juices were all around him on the tent floor, and his legs were quivering. *It's all over now but the cryin'.* I don't know what he was thinking in coming at me like that, but I feel as if it's a testament to his resolve. I wanted to be that fearless.

A couple of weeks later, some of my coworkers caught a scorpion and a camel spider, both about the same size. They placed them in the same small, empty aquarium. Although they are cousins, scorpions and camel spiders will fight one another if they feel provoked. There were some wagers about when the fight would start and which one would win. There was some stick poking to get them amped up. I don't know if they ever fought one another. I didn't hang around to watch.

Malaria preventive meds have a common side-effect of causing strange dreams and nightmares. Everyone at the base was required to take the meds because we were in a malaria prone area. In fact, one of my coworkers contracted the illness and had to be evacuated by medevac because he hadn't been taking his meds. I had some strange nightmares about that scorpion and camel spider fighting each other, even though I hadn't stuck around to watch. In my dreams, the scorpion always won.

I worked with another Vietnam-era Navy SEAL at that location. He and MC had served together in Nam. He was also new to the contract and a low man on the totem pole, like me. The other guys had given him the call sign "Pops," but I always referred to him as "Pappy" because, with his white beard and tobacco pipe clenched between his teeth, he reminded me of Poopdeck Pappy from the Popeye cartoons. He liked that I called him Pappy. He was from bayou country Louisiana and could cook a mean pot of gumbo.

Pappy had become an ordained Christian minister after he'd gotten out of the navy and became sort of an unofficial chaplain at our small base. I have since lost touch with him, but I still think about him sometimes and hope he's doing well. I thank God for the group Bible study sessions he organized. He always reminded us that no matter how evil an environment it seemed we were living and working in, God was looking out for us. He helped me keep my faith strong during a time when I might have started questioning it. Pappy and I had some great conversations about life and religion while standing overwatch shifts together.

I've worked with so many people over the years and many of the names and faces blend together, but Pappy is one of the good dudes I'll always remember.

We once escorted our section chief over to the other side of the camp, where the indigenous security forces lived. Our chief wanted to share some security-related information with the indigenous guard force commander. As we entered the Muslim commander's office we noticed a beautifully-decorated copy of the Koran prominently displayed on his desk. In an attempt to build rapport, our chief complimented the book's beauty and asked if it would be okay to pick it up and hold it for a moment.

"Are you a Muslim, sir?" the commander asked.

Our chief replied, "No. No, I'm not."

"Then I cannot allow you to touch the book. I'm sorry. It is against the rules."

He said it just like that. Pappy and I just looked at each other. I could tell we were both thinking the same thing. We talked about it later on at our next Bible study session. If it had been a beautifully-decorated copy of the Bible, it would not have made a difference who wanted to pick it up. The answer would have been, "Of course you may pick it up and hold it, my brother. All are welcome."

Hard-Skills Sustainment

I did a four-month rotation at that FOB, then spent four months home, then another four back at the FOB. Once a year, we had to attend what they called a "hard-skills sustainment course." The first one I attended was held at a training venue called Tactical Resource Center in Little Rock, Arkansas. It was November 2005. Arkansas in November is cold, wet, muddy, and slushy. It took me two weeks to perfect something the instructors referred to as "the rundown." It had to be performed in less than two minutes. The first time I attempted it, I thought it was impossible.

I had five M-4 magazines on my person. Each contained two rounds, so I only had ten rounds total. By the end of the rundown, eight of those rounds had to be in the center mass "A-box" of the human-shaped silhouette target. Two had to be in the target's head.

The drill started at the three-hundred-yard line with an empty H&K 416 rifle. When the instructor yelled "go" and started the timer, I had to do the hundred-yard dash to the two-hundred-yard line while loading my weapon with the first two rounds. Dropping into a prone position and trying to control my breathing in order to aim out at the target accurately was no easy task. My sights kept rising and falling. From two hundred yards, if you're off by a little, you'll miss by a lot. *One shot. Two shots.* Then I jumped up and dashed another hundred yards to the hundred-yard line while ejecting an empty mag and loading a new one. Now I had two more rounds. I dropped into a kneeling position. I learned to wear knee pads during the rundown so as not to bust my knees on the rocky Arkansas terrain.

Control your breathing. One shot. Two shots. I jumped to my feet and ran to the fifty-yard line, again reloading my weapon with two

fresh rounds. The shots from fifty yards and closer had to be taken while standing. I was getting close enough to see where my shots were landing. Eight shots all in the "A-box," so far. *I just need to get the two head shots. I still have plenty of time.*

As I ran to the seven-yard line and reloaded with my last two rounds, I forgot about the "twelve o'clock hold" rule. My rifle was sighted in from back at the fifty-yard line. The closer you get to your target, your sight picture naturally gets gradually higher because the bullet trajectory has changed a little. Bullets actually arc slightly as they travel out of the barrel. Gunfights are all about angles. I once heard a seasoned gunslinger describe a gunfight as "the ultimate game of angles." *The person who has the best possible angles will win.*

I put the red dot of my holographic sight right in the middle of the target's face. *One shot. Two shots.* "Time!" the instructor called. My two minutes were up

Those last two shots had dropped below the neckline, so they didn't count. The twelve o'clock hold got me. I should have put my red dot sight closer to the top of the target's forehead instead of the middle of its face. *I failed this run and only have one more chance to complete it. I was so close that time.* It's what real disappointment feels like. I was cold, wet, muddy, sore, exhausted, and had nothing to show for it.

The only thing I did differently on my very last attempt was I slowed down at the end and said a little prayer. I remembered my twelve o'clock hold. *Aim a little higher this time. Lord, let my arrows fly straight and true.* My last shot rang out at one minute and fifty-nine seconds. Eight rounds were center mass of the target, and the last two were right between the eyes. *I passed with one second to spare.*

There was another evolution, which consisted of taking multiple shots at a thin cardboard human-shaped silhouette target. The target would flip back-and-forth between facing the shooter and facing to the side. When it was flipped to the side, you weren't supposed to shoot. I was getting cocky. I shot at it when it was facing sideways and cut the target in half, just because I knew I could do it. The instructors were mad at me but also kind of impressed. They had never seen anyone do that before.

The shooting times on this hard-skills course were extremely fast, like nothing I'd seen before. I had always considered myself an above-average shot, but nothing like an expert. The beeps on the shot timer sounded as if they were going off with no time to spare between beeps. Sometimes, I was facing away from the target with my weapon pointed at the sky. *Beep.* I had to turn 180 degrees, bring my sights down on target and fire two head shots from the ten-yard line. *Beep.* That had to be done in less than two seconds. The more I did it, the better and faster I got.

In the category of least-favorite drills, I had to pretend my strong arm had been blown off and all I had was my support arm for applying a tourniquet, shooting, and reloading. It sounds impossible, but it can be done. They were trying to make us more ambidextrous. It felt clumsy though and took a lot of repetitions just to become mediocre at it.

"Again!" the instructors shouted. "Run it again!" Then it had to be repeated at night using night vision equipment. There were also transition drills, where our rifles would run empty, and we have no more mags to reload with. We had to quickly (and safely) sling the long guns out of the way. Then in the same motion, quickly draw our Glock pistols and accurately engage targets. We ran through the drills so many times that I was dreaming about them in my sleep. They made us disassemble our weapons and then put them back together in pitch-black darkness, using only night vision goggles. The NVGs throw off your depth perception.

My favorite drills were the stress courses we had to run, using the 40 mm grenade launchers and belt-fed machineguns. We were tactical weapons experts by the time the course was finished. It was rigorous, but I was having a blast (no pun intended). I was learning to use weapons I had never handled before, learning new skills, and getting paid to shoot someone else's ammo. Sometimes while deployed downrange, one of us might have to augment a helicopter crew by filling in as a door gunner. The pilots would take us up in the helo and hover over the shooting range, so we could practice engaging targets with a belt-fed machinegun from the air.

We brushed up on our door-breaching/room-clearing skills, and practiced performing emergency medical procedures on injured teammates. We shot from non-traditional shooting positions, from behind cover. We practiced extracting kidnapped principals from barricaded hostage situations. Our team got so we could perform these scenarios without taking any serious casualties to our team. That was the goal.

One of the most difficult, and yet most eye-opening modules of the training, was something called "mirror image." I felt like a nervous wreck by the time it was over. During the first couple of days, the instructors isolated, indoctrinated, and tried to brainwash us into thinking like the enemy. They tried to get us to think and act like terrorists; and to adopt their tactics, techniques, and procedures. The building blocks culminated in planning and carrying out simulated attacks on innocent civilians. It was all role-play, of course, but it was intense and they made it as realistic as possible.

Most special operators have to attend some variation of SERE (survival, evasion, resistance, and escape) school. This was not meant to be that, but they did expose us to certain aspects of it. The instructors who ran our mirror image block of instruction did a superb job, and I'm grateful to them for teaching me some new skills. *I hope I never meet any of them again in civilian life though, as I grew to dislike them more and more as the course went on.*

The instructors and role players could "attack" the students at any time during the course (simulated attacks with blanks and artillery simulators). They weren't supposed to be able to physically injure us. However, they did make us sign a waiver at the onset declaring we would not sue them if we did get hurt. Anyone not willing to sign the waiver would not be allowed to participate.

We were "attacked" at our bunkhouse in the middle of the night while we were sleeping. One of the role players would enter the bunkhouse by throwing a "flashbang" and firing blanks from an AK-47, reenacting an active-shooter scenario. The same thing happened while we were in the classroom watching a power point presentation. They "attacked" us again while we were eating breakfast in the chow hall. At no time during the course were we permitted to

let our guard down and no place was sacred; this was complete and intentional immersion training. They would even try to get us while we were taking showers or sitting on the toilet. Their favorite "attack" method was the simulated roadside bomb where they would "kill" us while driving between the bunkhouse, the dining facility, and the classroom.

This might all sound exciting at first, but it got really old after the first week. We got to where we just expected to be attacked all the time. I understood what they were trying to do, but it wasn't fun at all. You start to get burned out if you have to stay in a high state of alert for long periods of time like that. Your brain and body need periods of time where they can be totally relaxed in a safe place, so they can be recharged.

If you've ever played those brain teaser games, the people who design those things depend on something they call "cognitive bias." We see what we expect to see depending on several factors: who we are, what we believe, where we're from, and what we've experienced. When we get startled by a stimulus that alarms us, we go into fight, flight, or freeze mode. The reason our "life flashes before our eyes" is because our brain is tapping into hundreds of indicators from previous experiences. It's a survival instinct.

Well, I did that before and it worked; I lived through whatever the situation was. Is that going to work again in this instance; or am I going to die today?

This all happens in a split second.

Bad Monkey

My friend Brett goes by the call sign "Bad Monkey" or just "Monkey." He's a former Navy SEAL and one of the most solid operators I ever had the pleasure of working with. When we first started working together, I was curious about how he got his call sign, but I didn't want to come right out and ask. It didn't take long for me to figure it out. He was always doing something he shouldn't have been, just to try to make us laugh. Most people would describe him as "mischievous."

He and I were working a detail one time, and I referred to him as "Spoda." I was always trying to come up with original nicknames for people. Monkey said, "St. Nick, what does that mean?"

"Well, I figure you've been doing this job for a long time, and you're very wise. The newer guys are always coming to you for guidance, so you're kind of like Yoda in that regard. Right? But you're always doing something you ain't 'spoda' be doing." He liked that, and we both got a good laugh out of it.

We were all sitting around in the team room one time watching *The Big Lebowski*. We were killing time waiting for the last move of the day to return to base. No one was ever considered off-duty until everyone was safe and sound back at base. Even then, we weren't truly off-duty.

There was a restroom connected to our team room, but because the building was old and the ventilation was quite poor, we had a gentlemen's agreement. This particular restroom would be used for "number one" only. Otherwise, you would go back to your room and take care of it in your own bathroom.

This one guy was new to the base and went by the call sign "Hacker." He must have eaten something at dinner that didn't agree

with him, and I don't think anyone had explained the gentlemen's agreement to him yet. He quietly excused himself from the movie, and after a few minutes, we noticed a foul odor seeping into the team room.

Monkey looked over at the closed bathroom door. "Aw man, did Hacker go in there to take a…?" Monkey got out of his chair and walked over to one of the ammo cans where we kept the flashbangs.

For those unfamiliar with the *flashbang* (also known as "stun grenade"), it functions like a fragmentation grenade but is a non-lethal piece of ordnance. It has a pin you pull out and a spoon that releases. You throw it into a room, and after a few seconds, it goes off with a deafening bang and a blinding flash of light. The SWAT teams use them to surprise and disorient people, but flashbangs don't throw shrapnel the way frag grenades do, so they aren't likely to cause injuries.

Monkey walked over to the bathroom door with a flashbang in hand. He pulled the pin, kicked the door open, and tossed the device inside. Hacker was still on the toilet. Monkey yelled, "At least courtesy flush, you blue falcon!"

A "blue falcon" is a derogatory term for a guy who does something to screw his buddies over, also known as a "BF" or "bravo foxtrot." Hacker was screwing the whole team over, in this instance, by funking up the team room. He was the blue falcon that day.

We all knew what was coming next, so we plugged our ears with our fingers and closed our eyes. The stun grenade made a funny "tink tink tink" sound as it bounced across the tile bathroom floor, then came the loud bang and bright flash. Hacker was confused and disoriented for a few minutes, but he was okay. After he recovered, he was mostly just mad because we were all laughing uncontrollably. No one ever used the team room restroom for anything other than "number one" again.

Bad Monkey did and said things that bordered on getting him sent home, but because the base personnel liked him and he did a good job, everyone said, "Aw that's just Monkey being Monkey." Brett went on to write an excellent autobiography called <u>Pride</u>.

He and I participated in a real-life base evacuation once. There was a small remote base almost overrun by bad guys, so we had to go in and extract our personnel in a hurry. It was located smack-dab in the middle of bad guy territory. Monkey hates riding in helicopters because of a helo crash he was involved in, which he describes in his book. Actually, he describes it as more of a "hard landing" but it was a crash, nonetheless. *Any landing you can walk away from is a good landing.*

A new class of PMC candidates had begun its initial training at the BW facility in North Carolina. When word got back that we had executed our mission quickly, quietly, efficiently, and with zero casualties, they all cheered for us. It gave those new guys a sense of pride knowing they were gearing up to join our team.

You prepare a table before me in the presence of my enemies; you anoint my head with oil; my cup runs over.

The Lone Ranger

I definitely got to work with a cast of characters out there. When I talk about some of the places I've been, or things I've seen and done, people sometimes use the word *hero*. It humbles me because I don't see myself that way. I'm an average guy who has tried to do right by my God, my country, my family, and my community.

Whenever people use the term *hero*, I tell them that I've just been blessed. It seems as if I've always just been in the right place at the right time, and God has been looking out for me. I'm not a hero, but I have had the pleasure of working alongside a few. One of my personal heroes (and one of my best friends) is a guy I worked with often. He and I got stuck working some of the absolute worst details together. We call each other "brother."

Kris, call sign "Tanto," is a former Army Ranger best known for his actions in Benghazi, Libya, on September 11 and 12 of 2012. He is one of the coauthors of the book *13 Hours* and is the author of the autobiography *The Ranger Way*. Tanto worked as an advisor on the set of the movie <u>13 Hours</u>. His character was portrayed in the film by the much younger, much bigger, and much better-looking actor Pablo Schreiber. Pablo did a great job of capturing Tanto's personality.

Tanto and I were working a detail one time, and I did or said something to annoy him. We were always picking on each other just to entertain ourselves. We had been working many long hours and were both extremely tired. Plus, we were sick of looking at each other's ugly mugs. (His is uglier than mine, by the way.)

I don't remember what I did or said, but he responded with, "You know what, Nick? I don't even want to work with you anymore. I'd rather work by myself."

Off the top of my head, the only thing I could think to say was, "Well, then you wouldn't be Tanto anymore. You'd be The Lone Ranger." We both busted out laughing, and things were okay between us after that. *Kris doesn't spell his call sign the same as Tonto from* The Lone Ranger. *He spells it like a "tanto"-shaped blade.*

During our downtime, we had taken to binge watching *The Sopranos* in the team room. At some point during the series, I told him, "You know what, Kris? I'm like Tony Soprano in our relationship. You're more like the nephew, Christopher." He laughed and started calling me "Tony," or "Uncle Tony." He has more than a couple of different nicknames for me.

We were sitting in the team room watching an episode, and something I had eaten for lunch was not agreeing with me. Remembering the gentlemen's agreement, I knew I wasn't allowed to use the team room restroom. My room was a long walk, and I wasn't sure I'd be able to make it that far. Tanto's room was closer, so I asked him if I could use his toilet. He said, "Sure, bro. Just don't mess it up too bad in there."

"I promise I won't," I replied, and off I went.

As I mentioned earlier, the building we were living in was old. Sometimes, the electricity and plumbing did not cooperate. Sometimes, the utilities had a mind of their own. About the same time I finished my business and flushed Tanto's toilet, his hot water tank decided it wanted to cross into the cold water line and started filling the toilet tank with steaming hot water. Steam started emanating from the toilet tank and bowl. I casually walked back to the team room and asked, "Hey Kris, does your toilet always fill back up with scalding hot water?"

He looked at me with that Tanto look, as if he didn't know whether I was joking. "What are you talking about? Are you serious? What did you do?"

We ran back to his room, and steam was still steadily rising from the toilet. He yelled at me, "Bro, it's never done this before! You blew up my toilet! You took a mad poop! You dropped a nuclear turd in my toilet, bro! You're Tony, the Mad Pooper!"

I could not stop laughing as I ran to get the maintenance guy. He came over to Tanto's bathroom and knew how to fix it immediately. He had seen it happen in other restrooms on the base. Still, to this day, Tanto claims I tried to blow up his toilet by dropping a nuclear turd in it. He also still calls me "Tony the Mad Pooper" sometimes.

Tanto does and says some of the funniest things I've ever seen or heard. We were getting ready to go out on a QRF (quick reaction force) emergency call and were in the team room getting our gear on. Two former navy team guys, "Northman" and "Swanie," came running in at full sprint. Tanto yelled at the top of his lungs, "Holy crap, here comes SEAL Team Six! Everybody else can stand down! SEAL Team Six has got this! Everyone else just stay outta their way! Ha ha!"

I appreciated Tanto's sense of humor during those tense situations because it helped me calm down and regain my focus on what needed to be done. Some people did not appreciate it. Once we were in the vehicles and rolling, Tanto would be looking for a place to set his coffee cup down. He was always drinking coffee. Some armored vehicles had cup holders; some did not. If we were in one that did not, he would start yelling, "Why can't they put cup holders in these cars? This is a quarter-million-dollar vehicle! They couldn't have put one cup holder in it? Nick! Why didn't you get us one of the cars with a cup holder?" *He always knew how to lighten the mood and make me laugh.*

I was not with the team in Benghazi on that fateful night when the diplomatic outpost and annex were attacked. I was home with my wife and kids. Sometimes, I wish I had been out there with my brothers, but I also trust in God's plan for me. There must have been some reason why He didn't want me there. *Some of the guys made the ultimate sacrifice that night. I might well have been one of them, had I been there.*

I keep two books on my nightstand. One is my Bible. The other is a copy of Kris' book, The Ranger Way. My favorite paragraph from his book is this:

> Your perspective will shift if you can just let
> yourself be in a situation, even if it is the worst

situation in the world. If you can start by accepting your circumstances and think, "God, I am here. I am your vessel. What do you need me to do?" your world can open all the way up. Your mission will become clear. You can see and experience everything, take it all in, and begin to take action.

Marriott Bombing

In September 2008, I would be working out of the US embassy in Islamabad. Because we worked different deployment schedules, I had not seen my friend Scott in a couple of years. We would e-mail back and forth every month or so just to keep in touch, but I hadn't seen him in a while. Before I arrived in country, he e-mailed to let me know he would pick me up at the airport. It would be good to see Southside and work with him again.

Most of our work would consist of quickly and safely transporting US diplomats from point A to point B. Diplomats have to attend many meetings, official events, social functions, dinners, and so forth. Sometimes though, indigenous persons would claim to have information, which could possibly lead to locating some very bad dudes. Much of the information turned out to be garbage, but some of it was credible.

Our job as security contractors would be to physically search those people to make sure they were not carrying weapons or wearing suicide vests prior to meeting with a USG staff interviewer. It was the interviewer's job to come in and talk to the "walk-in" person to determine whether their information was credible. The contractors were the first line of defense; we were expendable. It was the nature of the job, and we accepted it.

When we weren't working, we liked to eat at two restaurants outside the embassy enclave. One was inside the Intercontinental Hotel; the other was in the Marriott. Both locations were access-controlled by indigenous security guards, so they seemed fairly secure. Scott and I had been driving around the city doing some shopping when we decided to have dinner at the Intercon.

As we waited for our food, we talked. He told me he had met a woman and was going to ask her to marry him. I told him I was happy for him, and it was time he found someone to settle down with. Scott also told me he wanted better job security. He was tired of the uncertainties that went along with contracting. We always described the contractor life as "musical chairs," in that you wanted to be seated in a chair when the music stopped.

"Cassie, I submitted my packet to go staff. You should consider it too, bro."

(Scott still called me Cassie, from the time we spent working together in Kosovo. He never took to calling me St. Nick.) He described all the advantages of getting hired on as a USG staffer. I told him I would think about it, but the idea of moving my family from Georgia to Virginia made me apprehensive. Staffers have to live in Northern Virginia, near Washington, DC. In my mind, that would be a major setback. It would also take some talking to Kim and the kids, and they would have to agree to it.

After we finished dinner, Scott and I stepped outside to head back to our car. It had just started to get dark out. All of a sudden, we saw a bright flash of light across the sky to our left. We thought it was lightning at first but then we heard the unmistakable delayed report of a large explosion. It sounded close.

Our team leader came over the radio, "All units return to base. All units return to base. There's been a report of a truck bomb detonation in the city."

We were only about a mile away from the embassy enclave, so we were back at our base in no time. We turned on the local news to find out what was being said about the explosion. Apparently, some bad dude had packed a dump truck full of explosives and had driven it right up in front of the Marriott Hotel. When the indigenous security guards told him to move the truck, he detonated himself. The explosion killed 54 people, injured 266, and left a 6 x 20 foot crater in front of the hotel. Major structural damage was done to the front of the building and the subsequent fire burned two-thirds of the hotel. The lobby and reception area were completely destroyed.

Scott and I looked at each other. All I could think to say was, "Well, I guess it's a good thing we ate dinner at the Intercon instead of the Marriott tonight."

It's all over now but the cryin'.

Tragedy at Khowst Base

A little more than a year later, in December 2009, the USG finally hired me on as a staff employee. I had talked to Kim and the kids, and they were okay with starting a new life in Virginia. It meant better job security, medical benefits, and a retirement plan. Our son, Nick, was twelve. Our daughter, Alex, was five.

Scott was about six months ahead of me in the hiring process; they'd hired him over the summer. When the government brought us onboard, the first thing they made us do was attend an antiterrorism action course (ATAC). At the end of the course, there would be a graduation ceremony where they would present us with official badges and credentials. Our family members would be invited to attend the ceremony.

In December 2009, I was getting ready to start my ATAC as Scott was getting ready to finish his. I went to the awards ceremony suite so I could see him graduate. I wanted to let him know that I was proud to be his friend. I also wanted to thank him for convincing me to submit my application packet. Once I got there, I realized he had already deployed on his first trip as a team leader. His bride was there to accept his badge and credentials on his behalf, so I got to meet her in person for the first time. She was seven months pregnant with their baby girl.

Apparently, the FOB in Khowst was short a team leader, so Scott had volunteered to leave early. That's the type of guy he was. Always willing to jump in and help whenever duty called. He would be there for Christmas and New Year's, then go home in February, in time for the birth of his daughter.

On the evening of December 30, 2009, I was on my way home from my training course. I was cursing Northern Virginia commuter

traffic, which is some of the worst in the world. I was still trying to adjust to it. I'd had a nice Christmas at home with Kim and the kids. It was the first time I'd been home for Christmas in years and was looking forward to New Year's Eve.

My cell phone rang and I immediately recognized the number. It was a fellow staffer, Dave, a guy I'd worked with overseas. He'd pushed my employment packet through the hiring process for me. I thought he was calling to wish me a belated Merry Christmas or early Happy New Year.

"What's up, Brother Dave?" I said as I answered the phone.

"Hey, did you hear about what happened in Khowst?"

"No. What happened?" *Scott.* (My thoughts immediately went to Scott because I knew he was at Khowst Base.)

"There was an explosion at the gate. Some of our guys got killed, including the new staffer."

"Who was it, Dave?" I asked, knowing full well what his answer would be.

"It was Southside."

I dropped my cell phone and pulled my car into the emergency lane. I felt as if I'd been punched in the gut. My friend was gone, and our career paths were so similar. I almost felt as though I'd been following in his footsteps. Then my thoughts went to his wife and how their daughter would now grow up without ever having met her daddy. After I got myself together, I drove home and hugged my wife and kids. The next thing I did was pick up the phone and call the deployment coordinator to find out how soon I could get back downrange, as I was looking to get some payback. *An eye for an eye.*

Later on, I found out that a source was supposed to have been bringing some important piece of information to the interviewers at Khowst Base. Scott and the security team had stopped the guy at the gate to search him. When Scott told him to remove his hands from his pockets, the subject detonated the suicide vest he was wearing, killing Scott along with several others.

I love the movie *Zero Dark Thirty*, but Southside's death is depicted during a scene in that film. Whenever it comes to that part, I have to fast forward past it to the next scene. Although it is a nec-

essary part of the movie and is based on what really happened, it hits too close to home for me.

For the Lord is close to the brokenhearted and saves those who are crushed in spirit.

The Protection of God

A s the RPG (rocket-propelled grenade) came flying toward my side of the helicopter, my life literally flashed before my eyes. It was pitch-black outside, so the helo crew was flying on NODs (night observation devices). The crew was short a door gunner, so I filled in on the starboard door gun. Through my NODs, I could see the RPG round sailing toward us. It came at us so fast; I didn't have time to call it out. We were conducting a routine drop off and pickup of personnel and had just taken off from the helipad. The downward thrust from the rotors must have caught the stabilizer fins on the rocket and caused it to change direction slightly. The rocket sailed under us, missing the helicopter skids by just a few feet.

All I could think to say was, "Did you guys see that?" into my headset microphone.

"Yep," I heard the pilot reply. "We're getting the heck out of here."

We never did see exactly where the rocket was launched from. I would have been all too happy to return fire.

I feel as though God held his protective hands around us that night. During the return flight back to base, I thought about all the times I'd had close brushes with death, but God protected me. *I wonder if a person gets only a certain number of those protections before they run out. I wonder if the number is different for each person. I wonder what my number is.*

I thought back to some of my earliest memories. When I was four, I tried to climb onto my dad's motorcycle by myself when no one else was around. It fell on top of me and pinned me to the ground. My dad was at work, but my mom heard me crying and ran out to the driveway. She lifted the motorcycle off me, by herself. I

was so young, I probably shouldn't have a memory of it, but I do. I believe people hang on to traumatic memories, no matter how young they were when the events took place.

During the return flight back to base, I started counting all of my close calls. There was also the time I almost drowned in my cousin's swimming pool when I was six. I didn't learn to swim until I was about eight, but I was bound and determined to swim in that pool. I was a stubborn kid who always wanted to accomplish impossible tasks on my own. I remember lying on the bottom of the pool like a sunken rock, looking up at the sunlight on the water's surface and thinking, *Wow this sucks. I wish I could breathe. I wish I was up there where the air is.* The water started to fill my lungs. and just when I was about to pass out, I saw my Uncle Mike breaking the surface of the water. He jumped in and pulled me out.

When I was eight, I was walking home from school with a group of friends. My house was only about six blocks from school, so I liked my mom to take me in the mornings, but I wanted to walk home with my friends in the afternoons. My house was farthest from the school, so one or two kids would drop out of the group as they got to their blocks, and I always wound up walking the last block alone.

One day as I was walking that last block by myself, some strange man came driving up beside me in a yellow Chevy Nova. He had his windows rolled down and said to me, "Hey, kid." I ignored him. He repeated, "Hey, kid. I lost my dog. Can you hop in my car with me and help me find him?"

I didn't say anything, just took off running toward my house, and I didn't stop running until I was on my front porch. The stranger sped away. My mom called the police, and they performed a courtesy check of the area, but they never did find the guy. *Lord only knows what he would have done to me, if I'd gotten into his car.*

When I was twelve, I was walking along the railroad tracks near our house. I was wearing headphones, jamming to music on my new Sony Walkman cassette player. Suddenly, I felt something like an invisible energy shoving me off the tracks. I also felt as if something was telling me, "Hey, dummy. Get off the tracks. Step to your left." As soon as I stepped left, clear of the tracks, a lone freight car came

rolling along from behind me. It was rolling slowly and quietly, but it surely would have crushed me like a little bug had I remained on the tracks. I later found out that some of the neighborhood kids had climbed up onto the freight car and knocked the handbrake off it, just to watch it roll away.

Kids will be kids, but that could have ended badly had God not been looking out for me that day.

Post-Traumatic Stress

After I'd seen more than a decade of deployments to third-world countries and war zones, the stress started to get to me. I believe post-traumatic stress (PTS) can be cumulative. There may not be one distinct event you can point to and say, "That was it." Also, different people experience it to varying degrees, so there's basically a PTS spectrum.

All the times I patted down subjects who could have been carrying weapons or wearing suicide vests, times I was awakened from a dead sleep to the sounds of incoming rocket and mortar explosions, emergency QRF call-ups, bad things I saw as a cop, close calls. The stress was bound to catch up with me sooner or later.

I started taking risks I normally would not have taken. Not with the lives of my teammates but with my own. I began to think I was invincible. Disregarding my own safety, I could feel myself getting progressively more reckless.

I was driving around by myself late one night in Peshawar, Pakistan. I was trying to teach myself to drive on the right-hand side of the car and the left-hand side of the road. Also, my issued car had manual transmission, so I was trying to get used to shifting with my left hand.

I rolled up on a police checkpoint. We had a deal with them. We were not supposed to have to "break seal," which meant I should not have had to roll the windows down or open the car doors. None of them spoke English anyway, and I didn't speak Pashto, so what were we going to talk about?

We were supposed to have been able to flash a diplomatic pass-port and our American consulate badge, and they were supposed to wave us through the checkpoints. If we had done something wrong, all

they had to do was call the consulate to find out who we were. I hadn't done anything wrong, but these cops were still not letting me through.

They kept pulling on the door handles, trying to get me to open the locked doors. They kept knocking on the windows and motioning for me to pull over to the side of the road. They started out just talking to me in Pashto, but their voices got gradually louder. Before I knew it, they were shouting at me. I wasn't going to break seal. One of them unholstered his pistol and started tapping on my window with the barrel. Another held his hand up in front of his face and started rubbing his fingers together, showing me the universal sign for money. They were so corrupt over there, and this situation was getting more intense by the second.

I liked it. I welcomed the challenge. I started to reach for my Glock. I was going to shoot them all through my car windows, starting with the one on my right. There were five of them altogether, surrounding my vehicle. The car I was driving that night was unarmored, what we would call a "thin skin."

One of them stepped out in front of me and leveled his AK-47 at my windshield. I threw the car into gear and stomped on the gas pedal. I left my pistol holstered for the moment and was just trying to drive off of the X. I almost hit the guy, but he jumped out of the way just in time. I could hear gunfire erupting from behind me as I sped away, but none of their rounds hit my car. Cops in third-world nations are horrible shots. Instead of using actual marksmanship skills and principles of shooting, they use the "spray and pray" technique. They may have been shooting into the air for all I knew; I didn't look back.

I'm fortunate they didn't chase me down though. They very well could've. I guess they figured it wasn't worth their effort. I could have been killed that night or, at the very least, thrown into a local jail. *Sometimes when I reflect on all the crazy things I've done, I'm surprised I'm still alive.*

Eventually, I started feeling classic symptoms of PTS: depression, anxiety, hypervigilance, paranoia, extreme mood swings, irritability, social isolation, flashbacks, nightmares, guilt, loneliness, insomnia, emotional detachment, and self-destructive thoughts. I

thought I could handle those feelings on my own. I thought asking for help would be seen as weakness.

At home between deployments, I didn't feel I fit in; didn't even feel as if I belonged there anymore. All I wanted was to get back overseas with my teammates because that's where I felt like I fit in. All my wife and kids wanted was their old husband and daddy back. I was growing distant from my family and friends, and worse, growing distant from God. I stopped reading my Bible, stopped going to church, stopped blessing my meals, and stopped praying.

I didn't want to die, I never wished for it, but I also didn't care whether I lived. I would ride my motorcycle at extreme speeds without wearing a helmet. Alone in my Dodge Charger, I would dart in and out of traffic at dangerous speeds after removing my seatbelt. I was becoming an adrenaline junkie.

I never drove drunk, but if I was home and not going anywhere for the rest of the evening, I would binge drink beer and liquor. I wouldn't say I was an alcoholic, but I was definitely not sober. I felt as if drinking helped me distance myself from reality and numbed the pain I was feeling inside. I lost hours at a time, blacked-out drunk. People told me things I couldn't recall doing or saying. I wasn't myself. I was on autopilot and didn't like who I was becoming. I was out of control and took a "leave me alone" attitude toward my family and friends. Unfortunately, I alienated myself from many of them and didn't care that I was doing it. I regret it now.

What do our adversaries and enemies attempt to exploit when they come? Weaknesses and vulnerabilities, such as life crisis (who hasn't had one), substance abuse, disgruntlement, loneliness, and financial stress. They'll look for a couple of things that make you vulnerable and then they'll try to make you their victim. You must make yourself into the hardest target possible.

The more I thought about this, the more it seemed like exactly the kind of thing Satan would do. He's the Ultimate Enemy. He will approach you when you're at your lowest and then give you his pitch: "Hey, I can fix this. I can fix this for you, but you have to do something for me in return."

As I was pondering this, my mom called to say that my Uncle Charlie had been killed when a train struck his car at a road crossing. He was the middle brother on my dad's side, between my dad and Uncle Mike. Apparently, he was trying to drive around the flashing railroad drop arms to beat the train. It was ruled an accident, but I still wonder if he didn't commit suicide by train. Uncle Charlie was mentally and emotionally unstable. He struggled with anxiety and depression his whole life and had talked about how inferior and worthless he felt at times. I had not seen or talked to him in years, and now he was gone. We were close when I was younger but grew apart as I got older. *I feel sorry for people who say they've never felt God move in their life.* Now I would never get a chance to say goodbye to him.

I finally decided enough was enough. I started reading my Bible and praying again. I started going to church and talking to my pastor again. I asked God for forgiveness and tried to make amends as best I could to family members and friends I had hurt. During my spare time, I started running and lifting weights again and spent a lot of time at the shooting range to sharpen my skills. I found beer and liquor a huge waste of my money, time, energy, and talent, so I quit drinking and tried to live as clean as possible. When I was forty-one-years old, I felt as good as I did at twenty-one. I was lean, mean, and at the top of my game again. Then it all came crashing down.

Fall from Grace

By August of 2014, I was getting ready to turn forty-two. It was time for me to attend sustainment training again, prior to heading out for my next deployment. I was confident that it would not be an issue. *It's just a box I need to check before I head out, that's all.* I was in great physical shape, had been spending a good bit of time at the gym and the shooting range, and had been practicing my room-clearing tactics.

Over the year leading up to this, several changes had taken place within the administrative offices in Virginia. It was too much change, too fast, which is hardly ever a good thing. Upper management had seen fit to close down several of our satellite offices to save money. This turned my fifteen-minute commute into an hour-plus, which I was not happy about, but I would be back overseas soon, where I wouldn't have to worry about the commute.

The chief and deputy chief of our unit, Joe and Todd, retired at the same time. Those guys were seasoned veterans of the unit, with years of overseas protective experience between them. They made their way up through the ranks, as I was trying to do. I had a ton of respect and would have served with either of them anywhere in the world. I would have taken a bullet for them.

They were replaced by two women (for the purpose of this book, I will refer to them as "Anastasia" and "Drizella," like Cinderella's stepsisters). The new chief and deputy chief had a lot of administrative and managerial skills but zero field experience. They had never done our job. They'd never even been through any of our training or vetting courses, yet Anastasia and Drizella would be running the unit now. They were political appointees, and they were good managers, but not good leaders. They had no business filling those positions,

in my opinion. None of the guys in the office were happy about them being in charge, except for a handful of booty-kissers. I've never sucked-up to anyone in my life and wasn't about to start now.

I have no problem with women supervising me, but I do think they should have at least gone through the same training I have and should have had at least some field experience doing the job. These two ladies came from budget and finance backgrounds. They had no clue what went on in the field. I figured I'd give it six months and see how things went. I would go to my training course, then do a two-month deployment, then come home for a month, then do another two-month deployment. If I wasn't happy with the way things were going after this, I'd look for a new job. That was my plan.

How bad can it be? I thought. *I'm a field service officer. They're just out-of-touch upper management. They sit in the front office. It's going to be okay.* It didn't take long for me to realize I was wrong. It was not going to be okay.

I reported to the training center the last week of August 2014. I was ready to get this done so I could get back to my family for the long weekend. It was the week before Labor Day. The course would take five days to complete, and the very first evaluated event was on Monday morning. It was the PT test: push-ups, pull-ups, sit-ups, obstacle course, distance run, and a fifty-meter drag of a 180-pound sand-filled dummy. It was an objective event, in that you had to achieve a certain score within a specified time limit. Most of the other events during the week, such as weapons qualifications and stress courses, would also be objective.

There was only one event that would be subjective, in that it was left up to the lead evaluator's discretion whether you passed or failed. That would be the close quarters battle (CQB). I was anxious to get it over with, but they would save it for last. When I saw who the lead evaluator was, I could not believe my eyes. It was the same guy who had been a BW evaluator ten years prior—the one who said I flagged my partner when I didn't. (For the purpose of this book, I'll give him the call sign "Moxie.")

When he came into the classroom to introduce himself on the first morning, he said, "I'm Moxie, and I'm the new "shot-caller"

here at the training center. That means I'm the one who says whether you stay or go. I say whether you get a thumbs up (pass) or a thumbs down (fail). Management hangs on every word I say, so don't piss me off."

I pulled one of the instructors aside, one of the guys I knew and trusted from having served with downrange. I asked him, "Dude, what's Moxie doing here?"

"Anastasia and Drizella hired him. He's one of the new changes they made to the training program. I guess they felt like the sustainment course wasn't hard enough before, so they brought him over. Just a heads up, bro, he does not like ex-cops. He only wants former military out here and doesn't believe former law enforcement should be working with us."

"But I've been doing this job for more than a decade," I said.

"Doesn't matter, bro. He'll hone in on something he doesn't like about you and cut you out of the herd just because you're not prior military. I, and the other instructors out here, have seen him do it. None of us like him. And he's telling the truth when he says that Anastasia and Drizella hang on every word he says. They do."

Great. Just great. My hopes of passing this course were starting to dwindle, but I tried to maintain a positive attitude. I said a silent prayer prior to each event: *Trust in the Lord with all your heart, and do not lean on your own understanding.*

We went out to the obstacle course to perform the PT test. I completed it within the required time limit. However, I did feel a slight spasm in my lower back as I was dragging the dummy. I was cautious and trying to use the proper form. I had thrown my lower back out previously while doing a high-intensity interval workout. I had to do six weeks of physical therapy and did not want it to happen again. I sailed through every objective over the course of the week with solid scores and well under the required time limits. The final milestone event I needed to pass was on Friday. It was the CQB evaluation.

Moxie kept making me run through the "kill-house" scenarios over and over while he was passing everyone else. "Cassel," I would hear him say from up on the catwalk. "That was a thumbs down. Run it again."

He wasn't even being specific about what I needed to fix. He kept saying, "That run just didn't look very good. Go again." I asked him during one of the runs to please be specific about what I was doing wrong. He said, "You flagged your partner."

I felt like I was stuck in a nightmare. My thoughts went back to 2004, ten years prior, when he had falsely accused me of flagging my partner at the BW training facility. I had come full circle. *I know for a fact that I did not "flag my partner," but it won't do any good to argue with him. He's the shot-caller.*

I realized at that moment, no matter how perfectly I cleared the house; Moxie was not going to pass me. Other students were making more mistakes and worse mistakes than I was, but he was passing them. After the last scenario, he could tell I was exhausted and getting frustrated. I was tired of being placed in no-win situations and getting shot up with sim rounds by the other instructors. I was ready to punch him. I got tunnel vision as he spoke to me, but I held back. I prayed for peace to come over me, and it did.

Moxie told me he was going to recommend to upper management that I attend remedial CQB training prior to heading out for my next deployment. He told me that whenever this had happened to other guys, the front office always let them make up just this portion of the course, as opposed to making them do the whole week over again. *Since I already passed all the other milestone events, I should only have to do a couple days of remedial CQB and be good to go. That doesn't seem so bad.*

I grudgingly accepted Moxie's recommendation and drove home. I was frustrated, not with myself, but with the situation. It seemed arbitrary and counterproductive. During the drive home, I found myself looking forward to spending Labor Day weekend with Kim and the kids. I was also starting to think about other jobs I could apply for. At one time, I was seen as one of the top field officers, and now I meant nothing to them. The new managers were ready to throw me out…like yesterday's garbage.

Every tongue which rises against you in judgment, you shall condemn.

Front Office Decision

When I returned to the office the Tuesday after Labor Day, the front office had already made a decision. *Wow, that was fast.* The managers decided, in their infinite wisdom, that I should complete the entire week-long revalidation course over again. They told me if I did not pass all the training events on my second attempt, I would have to cancel my upcoming deployment and attend the month-long basic course again. I felt like a seasoned veteran getting busted back to boot camp for falling out on a PT run. It didn't make a bit of sense to me. I politely questioned their decision and was told, "It's a new policy we're implementing."

Uh-huh. A new policy, starting with me. I guess I'm the guinea pig. I didn't argue with management's decision. Like any good soldier, I followed my orders. I drove back out to the training center the following week, fully willing to complete the week-long course again, starting from square one. My lower back was not cooperating this time though. Monday morning, when I was dragging the 180-pound dummy for the PT test, the muscles in my back spasmed, and I had to drop the dummy just short of the fifty-meter requirement. Moxie actually laughed at me and threatened to send me home if I couldn't complete the task. I tried to make the point that I had passed this portion of the course just two weeks prior, but he wasn't willing to discuss it. He sent me home.

During the drive home, I decided that I would not be going through the month-long basic course again. I was in my early thirties the first time I went through, and it was hard enough then. Now I was in my early forties, and it took my body longer to recover from injuries. I might very well go through the month of abuse, only to

have the shot caller fail me for some subjective and arbitrary thing right at the end. I wasn't doing that again.

Also, reality was setting in. I was getting older and could no longer do some of the things I used to. If I couldn't drag a 180-pound injured protectee or teammate to safety without my back muscles spasming, maybe I didn't need to do protective work anymore. I would look for a new job within the government. I would ask upper management to work with me and allow me a reasonable amount of time to find a new job. I considered it the least they could do for all the years of service I'd given them.

Once I got home, I saw my primary-care physician to address some injuries I sustained during the training course. He was going to have me attend physical therapy sessions for my back again, but he also conducted a full physical, including blood work. When the results came back, the doctor noticed my creatine kinase levels were unusually high. He said it could have been caused by muscle inflammation from some of the injuries I'd sustained, but he wanted me to follow up with a neurologist for additional testing.

After running more tests over the next couple of weeks, the neurologist diagnosed me with a form of muscular dystrophy. Other than watching the Jerry Lewis MDA telethon every year on TV, I didn't know much about it. I didn't know there were different forms. Those people I saw on TV were usually little kids in wheelchairs. The doctor explained it's a genetic disorder, inherited from one of my parents. I later found out it runs in my mom's side of the family. I was born with it, but the doctor explained that some forms don't manifest until middle age. It's a mutated gene, which prevents the body from making the proteins necessary for healthy muscles. It causes progressive weakness and loss of muscle mass, and there's currently no cure. Mine is called FSHD (facioscapulohumeral dystrophy). I sat in disbelief for a few minutes. I didn't know what to say.

I started to feel as if God had turned His back on me, or taken His protection away, and I didn't know why. *Lord, why have you forsaken me? Why are you so far from saving me, so far from my cries of anguish? I've tried to do right by you.*

I thought about going back to binge drinking, but I didn't. It would've been easy to have gone back to potentially self-destructive behaviors, but I didn't. Now when I think back on it, it scares me to think about what I might have been capable of. I felt truly worthless, like I had no purpose anymore.

As I sat in church on Sunday, listening to my pastor's sermon, the answer came to me. It was as if God Himself was speaking to me. The pastor quoted C. S. Lewis from that interview I'd read years ago, when I was first discovering my faith. The one where the interviewer asked, "Why do you think the righteous suffer?"

Lewis replied, "Why shouldn't they suffer? They're the only ones who can handle it."

I am the righteous, and I can handle it. Thank you, God. Thank you.

The whole situation, even though it seemed dark and grim there for a while, was actually a blessing. My entire perspective changed to a positive outlook, like flipping a switch. I was moved to tears sitting in church, as I looked over at Kim and our two beautiful children.

I'd be working regular hours now, and off on weekends and holidays. I would be home for birthdays and anniversaries, which hadn't been the case for too many years. I'd have an opportunity to make up for lost time with Kim and the kids. Even though the kids were eleven and seventeen now, there was still time to bond with them before they left the nest. Kim wouldn't have to worry about me anymore, like she did when I was deployed overseas.

This isn't a time for self-pity, this is a time to celebrate. I trust you, Lord, with my uncertainties, for you take away my fears and doubts. I trust in your plan for me. I trust you more than I trust myself.

Afterword

G od bless you all for giving me the opportunity to serve and protect you. For trusting me with your safety and security, I can never thank you enough. I'm humbled. It has been the greatest honor of my life. When I reflect on the challenges, and the highs and lows, I have very few regrets. The one thing that always got me through every situation was faith: faith in my God, faith in my country, and faith in my family and friends. Thank you for taking the time to read my stories. I hope you enjoyed them, and I pray that something I've written here touched you or stuck with you or can help you in whatever you may be going through.

I'll leave you with this. It's important to me, so I'll share it with you. One of my favorite movies is *The Book of Eli,* and one of my favorite prayers is the one Denzel Washington speaks in the final scene:

> Dear Lord, thank you for giving me the strength and the conviction to complete the task you entrusted to me. Thank you for guiding me straight and true through the many obstacles in my path. And for keeping me resolute when all around seemed lost. Thank you for your protection and for your many signs along the way. Thank you for any good that I may have done. I'm so sorry about the bad. Thank you for the friend(s) I made. Please watch over (them) as you watched over me. Thank you for finally allowing

me to rest. I'm so very tired. But I go now to my rest at peace, knowing that I have done right with my time on this earth. I fought the good fight. I finished the race. I kept the faith.

About the Author

John "St. Nick" Cassel is a former police officer and US government security contractor who has been deployed to the Balkans, South Central Asia, and the Middle East. He currently lives in Virginia with his wife and two children. This is his first novel. Please follow John on Instagram, @john.st.nick.